# EMPLOYERS AND THE LAW:
## 2013–14 Anthology of Best Articles

George J. Siedel and John V. Siedel

Editors

Published by Van Rye Publishing, LLC
www.vanryepublishing.com

ISBN-10: 0-9903671-3-4
ISBN-13: 978-0-9903671-3-0

# CONTENTS

## IV. SPECIFIC TOPICS

# Preface

The law touches almost every aspect of the relationship between employers and their employees. Hundreds of articles are written every year about legal developments that impact this relationship. This anthology is a compilation of the best of these articles that were written between March 1, 2013 and February 28, 2014. This time frame was selected because it enabled us to include end-of-year articles that review key changes in the law during 2013 and beginning-of-year articles that cover trends and action items for 2014.

The articles in this collection were written by leading US employment law experts. In selecting these articles the goal was to include articles that are concise, clearly-written, practical and relevant to the responsibilities of business owners, managers, and human resource professionals—and to their legal advisors.

The result is a mixture of two types of articles. Some articles focus on fundamental, recurring legal concerns. These include, for example, articles on employer responsibilities relating to holiday activities, off-duty conduct, record keeping, reductions in force, retaliation, seasonal workers, severance agreements, trade secrets, and workplace violence.

Other articles address issues that have recently received national attention as a result of changes in the business and legal environment. These include articles on employer responsibilities relating to criminal background checks, Bring Your Own Device policies, workplace bullying, electronic communications, "leaning in," obesity, social media, telecommuting, and workplace wellness programs.

While authored by leading experts in the field of employment law, these articles are published only for educational and informational purposes to give you a general understanding of the law. They are not intended and should not be construed as legal advice.

The articles are organized into four groupings.

***Opening Test.*** Do you have a sound understanding of the legal responsibilities of employers? Before using the resources presented in this book, we suggest that you first answer the ten questions posed by Anthony J. Romano and Scott M. Gilbert in the opening article entitled "New Year's Resolution—Protecting Your Business: 10 Employment Law Questions to Test Your Knowledge." Congratulations if you can answer eight or more of these questions correctly!

***Broad Coverage.*** With the onset of a new year, several authors wrote review articles that summarize legal developments in 2013 and agendas for 2014. For example, in "An Employer's 'Top 5' Action Items for 2014," Frank C. Morris, Jr. reviews key employment law actions for 2014, such as reviewing mandatory arbitration agreements, enhancing accessibility of websites to individuals with disabilities, ensuring that job descriptions have been updated, and reviewing confidentiality and non-compete agreements.

The focus of Harold P. Coxson's article "A Review of Labor and Employment Policy in 2013: What's Next in 2014" is on Congressional and government agency developments in 2013 and anticipated regulatory actions in 2014 relating to, for example, proposed revisions to the "persuader activity" reporting requirements and implementation of the Occupational Safety and Health Administration ("OSHA") Injury and Illness Prevention Program.

In "Your 14 Labor and Employment Resolutions for 2014," Alizah Z. Diamond discusses fourteen key labor and employment issues that will impact employers in 2014. These concerns include, for example, the impact of the Affordable Care Act, minimum wage increases, and the need to update employee handbooks.

"Welcome 2014: Five Employment Law Trends You Need to Know" by Kristin L. Oliveira covers the impact of "Ban the Box" laws on your workplace, employee wellness plans, the use of Facebook and other social media websites in making hiring decisions, the need for a BYOD policy, and developments relating to independent contractors.

***Global Concerns.*** In today's global business world, employers are increasingly concerned with the legal environment outside the United

States. In her article "14 Global Workplace Trends for 2014," Ute Krudewagen addresses the fourteen top legal trends that impact multinational employers in 2014. These trends include legal concerns relating to global competition for talent, a stronger need to protect confidential information, new discrimination and gender equality laws, and a global focus on anti-corruption measures.

Two articles by Donald C. Dowling, Jr. address specific employment law concerns that extend outside the United States. In "Individual Employment Dismissal Obligations Outside the US," he inventories seven types of dismissal laws that employers might encounter overseas that fall within three categories: (1) dismissal procedures, (2) pre-termination notices and (3) severance and wrongful termination awards.

In "Cross-Border Age Discrimination Compliance," Mr. Dowling addresses one of the toughest issues in developing an international equal opportunity compliance initiative—age discrimination. After summarizing the nature of the problem and the challenge in developing a cross-border discrimination policy, he provides a four-step solution for bringing international age discrimination initiatives into compliance.

***Specific Topics.*** Most of the articles in the book cover specific topics relating to the legal responsibilities of employers. As noted earlier, some of these articles address longstanding concerns for employers while other concerns have recently gained prominence.

*Background Checks*. In "And by the Way, Are You a Criminal," Andria Ryan poses three key questions that employers should ask to ensure that hiring and screening practices are not discriminatory. While the article is directed toward the hospitality industry, the advice is also relevant to other types of employers.

*Bring Your Own Device*. BYOD policies offer employers an opportunity to significantly reduce IT costs and give employees the freedom to choose the type of device they want. However, as discussed by Zachary B. Busey in "BYOD—Bring Your Own Device Policies," these policies raise a number of legal concerns and the need for an up-to-date company policy.

*Bullying.* Workplace bullying achieved national prominence and heavy media coverage as a result of allegations by a Miami Dolphins football player. Linda Bond Edwards and Brent D. Hartman, in their article "When the Playground Bully Becomes an Adult Workplace Bully," discuss the types of workplace behaviors that constitute bullying and provide suggestions on how employers should address bullying.

*Confidential Information.* With an increase in trade secret theft in recent years, employers should understand key concepts. In "Guidelines for Protecting Company Trade Secrets," Armand J. Zottola and Robert F. Parr provide practical advice on how to identify and protect trade secret information.

*Defense of Marriage Act.* Section 3 of DOMA defined marriage for purposes of federal law as the union of a man and a woman. In *United States v. Windsor*, the US Supreme Court held that this section is unconstitutional. Robert A. Fisher and Lyndsey M. Kruzer, in "Supreme Court Finds DOMA to Be Unconstitutional—Impact on Employers Explained," discuss a number of significant changes as result of this decision. These changes relate to employee benefits, family emergencies, immigration, etc.

*Electronic Communications.* The widespread use of Twitter has resulted in a new word describing a legal claim for a libelous post—"twibel." In "She Tweeted What?!" Tony G. Puckett discusses measures that employers should take to prevent such claims, including training programs that utilize specific examples and a social media policy that describes in detail what is and is not permitted in social media posts.

*Employee Leaves.* While most employers are familiar with the basics of the laws relating to employee leaves, some types of leave create unique challenges. Carolyn D. Walker, in "FMLA Leave or ADA Accommodation (Or Both)? Overview of Beyond the Basics," describes six of these thorny situations and provides clear guidance on how to handle them.

*Family Responsibilities Discrimination.* In *Lean In: Women, Work, and the Will to Lead*, author Sheryl Sandberg, Chief Operating Officer at Facebook, notes that she teaches managers to encourage employees to discuss family matters. Do such discussions create discrimination litigation risks? In "Does Leaning In Make Legal Sense for Employers? Definitely," John P. Furfaro, Risa M. Salins and Anne E. Villanueva conclude that greater risks might lie in not engaging employees on these issues.

*Flu Planning*. Recurring legal questions that arise during flu season, such as workplace policies regarding "presenteeism," the legality of flu vaccine requirements, and employer rights and responsibilities under the Americans with Disabilities Act are reviewed by Joseph J. Lynett in "Plan to Minimize Spread of Flu and Legal Risks in the Workplace during Flu Season."

*Health Insurance Portability and Accountability Act*. The "Omnibus Rule" amending HIPAA took effect in March 2013 and made several key changes in privacy and security rules. In "HIPAA and the Omnibus Rule: How to Assess Whether and What Your Company Must Do to Comply," Helen A. Christakos enumerates these changes and describes what covered companies must do to comply with the new rule.

*Holidays*. Unique liability concerns arise during holidays, such as using appropriate holiday decorations, accommodating religious practices, educating employees about holiday gift exchanges, and awareness of legal issues relating to holiday parties. Stephanie Leach summarizes these concerns in "Avoiding Holiday Liability for Employers."

*Independent Contractors*. Employers who misclassify employees as independent contractors face a number of legal risks, including unpaid overtime, unpaid taxes, workers' compensation concerns, and discrimination claims. In "Employee vs. Independent Contractor: What You Need to Know," Roger Royse describes the differences between employees and independent contractors and why the distinction is important.

*Lactation Discrimination*. Employers who fail to accommodate nursing employees face several possible legal claims, such as sex discrimination and retaliation. In "New Developments Surrounding Lactation Discrimination," Sarah Andrews and Sarah E. Bouchard discuss these claims and measures that employers can take to reduce the risk of liability.

*Obesity.* The recent adoption by the American Medical Association of a policy that labels obesity as a disease that requires medical intervention for treatment and prevention has increased the likelihood that courts will consider obesity as a disability under the Americans with Disabilities Act. In "Obesity as a Disability Under the ADA: Is It More Likely Now Than Before," Cherie Blackburn describes the impact on employment decisions and actions.

*Off-Duty Conduct.* Can you withdraw a job offer after an applicant tests positive for marijuana prescribed by her doctor when the prescription is legal under state law? In "You Can't Fire Me For That—I Was Off Duty!" Jeffrey A. Dretler provides examples of off-duty conduct that, depending on state law, might be grounds for discipline or termination by employers, such as the use of tobacco, alcohol—and medical marijuana.

*Privacy.* Recent activity at both the federal and state levels has led to increased focus on securing company information to protect privacy. In "Protecting Your Business with Strong Operational Privacy Controls," Paul Glist, Christin S. McMeley and Daniel P. Reing provide examples of this government activity, along with a list of specific questions that a broad spectrum of company departments should address to secure data.

*Records.* Certain basic documents often determine the outcome of employment litigation. In "Five Documents Sure to Appear in Your Lawsuit," Mauro Ramirez describes the "Big Five" that can make or break your case: job descriptions, handbooks, performance evaluations, disciplinary documents and responses to administrative charges.

*Reductions in Force.* Reductions in force can trigger expensive litigation and liability. While in some cases RIFs might be unavoidable, employers can adopt guidelines to reduce liability risks. These guidelines, along with alternatives to RIFs, are discussed in "How to Control a Reduction in Force" by James R. Wiley.

*Retaliation.* Retaliation is a word that should strike fear in the heart of every employer, as it is the most frequently filed charge with the Equal Opportunity Employment Commission ("EEOC"). Richard B. Cohen provides "A Refresher Course for Employers on Retaliation" that includes a three-part definition of retaliation and advice on retaliation claims prevention.

*Religious Discrimination.* Daniel H. Handman examines the challenges that employers face when religious practices conflict with workplace requirements in "Three Questions Employers Should Ask About Religious Accommodation Requests." These questions relate to whether an employee's bona fide religious belief conflicts with an employment duty, whether an accommodation imposes an undue hardship and whether any reasonable accommodations are available.

*Seasonal Employees.* A wide range of legal issues arise when businesses hire seasonal workers—such as wage and hour issues, hiring students, at-will employment, record-keeping rules and onboarding concerns. These issues are explored in "Seven Employment Topics to Consider When Hiring Seasonal Workers" by Steven F. Pockrass.

*Severance Agreements.* Severance agreements are commonly used by employers to obtain a release from liability from departing employees. In "Avoiding Pitfalls of Severance Agreements," Rachelle E. Hill discusses several legal issues that employers should consider when using these agreements, including waivers of future claims, compliance with the Older Workers Benefit Protection Act, and requirements when there is a termination of multiple employees.

*Sexual Discrimination.* In "Title VII Does Not Cover Sexual Orientation… Or Does It?" T. Harold Pinkley discusses a recent EEOC ruling that a claim of "gender identity, change of sex and/or transgender status" is covered by Title VII, and he provides a list of steps that prudent employers should take to avoid liability. These steps include revising HR policies and reviewing pre-employment background checks.

*Social Media.* Do you have an agreement with your employees addressing ownership of social media accounts? Have you provided them with clear guidance regarding the use of these accounts? These topics are addressed, along with a discussion of case law, in "Ownership of Business-Related Social Media Accounts" by Aaron Rubin and Anelia V. Delcheva.

*Telecommuting.* Technology changes that define the workplace were widely discussed following CEO Marissa Mayer's decision to ban telecommuting at Yahoo!. In "How Flexible Are You? Stretching the Boundaries with a Remote Workforce," Laura Hayward and Brian Morris discuss legal complications in developing your telecommuting policy, such as providing reasonable accommodation, protecting sensitive data and complying with wage and hour regulations.

*Wellness.* In "Workplace Wellness Programs," John B. Brescher, Jr., Mark A. Daniele, Joel E. Horowitz, Jane S. Kimball and Eleanor D. Thompson discuss new Workplace Wellness Program regulations that are designed both to prevent discrimination and to ensure that employers understand the general requirements governing these plans.

*Workplace Violence.* It is increasingly important for employers to understand workplace violence. In "Workplace Violence Examined," Kelly O. Scott first defines the four Occupational Safety and Health Administration (OSHA) categories of violence and describes who is at risk under each category, and then discusses workplace security measures.

* * *

We hope that the resources in this book will help you achieve business success in a responsible manner. If you have specific questions or need additional information, the authors have provided contact information at the end of each article.

# I. OPENING TEST

# Chapter 1

## New Year's Resolution—Protecting Your Business: 10 Employment Law Questions to Test Your Knowledge

by Anthony J. Romano and Scott M. Gilbert*

The New Year has arrived, and what better way to thaw out from the "Polar Vortex" than by settling in with a warm cup of cocoa and reviewing the answers to our Employment Law New Year's Quiz.

1. An employee has complained that he has been working long hours recently, but has not received any overtime pay. The employee is paid a salary and not hourly, so the company:

   a. Can ignore the employee's complaint because salaried employees are not entitled to overtime.

   b. Should offer the employee "comp time" to compensate him for the extra work.

   c. Should take steps to confirm that the employee is properly classified as "exempt" under the Fair Labor Standards Act and any applicable state laws.

**ANSWER:** **C**. Paying an employee a salary does not necessarily mean that the employee is exempt from the overtime requirements of the FLSA. For example, in addition to receiving a minimum weekly salary of $455, to qualify under one of the "White Collar Exemptions" an employee's job duties must also fit within the scope of exception claimed. Additionally, private employers cannot use "comp time" in lieu of overtime pay. Consequently, the employer here should take the complaint seriously and exercise due diligence to ensure that it is compliant with the FLSA.

2. The U.S. Supreme Court's decision in *U.S. v. Windsor* struck down a portion of the Defense of Marriage Act of 1996, which barred federal recognition of same-sex marriage. In light of this recent Supreme Court ruling, health and welfare benefits provided under an employer sponsored benefit plan must:

   a. Be extended to all same-sex spouses of employees regardless of the terms of the plan document.

   b. Be extended to all same-sex spouses of employees who reside in states that recognize same-sex marriage, and to registered domestic partners in those states that do not recognize same-sex marriage.

   c. Be extended to only those spouses that meet the criteria as a "spouse" as that term is defined under the controlling benefit plan document.

**ANSWER:** **C**. While the Employee Retirement Income Security Act ("ERISA") requires that retirement plans extend certain benefits to spouses of eligible plan participants, ERISA does not mandate that employer sponsored health and welfare plans provide coverage to spouses of eligible employees. Because of this, neither same-sex nor opposite-sex spouses are required to be offered coverage under an employer's self-insured medical plan. Under an insured plan, the terms of the policy will control whether spouses must be offered coverage. Notwithstanding the fact that current law does not mandate spousal health and welfare benefits, employers that wish to provide coverage only to spouses of the opposite sex should first consider the legal ramifications and potential discrimination claims that could be brought by employees with same-sex spouses.

3. An employee has developed a medical condition that requires him to take a leave from work. He has now used all of his allotted leave under the Family and Medical Leave Act, and he is not entitled to any other leave pursuant to any company policy. However, the employee needs more time to recover and has requested some additional leave. In response to this request, the company:

a. Should inform the employee that he has used all of the leave to which he is entitled under the FMLA, and that his employment is terminated as a result, but that he is free to reapply when he is able to fully return to work.

b. Should inform the employee that it will try to keep his position open if possible, but that if a qualified candidate is found before he is able to return to the job, he will be replaced.

c. Should treat the employee's request for additional leave as a request for an accommodation under the American's with Disabilities Act and evaluate in good faith whether the request can be granted.

**ANSWER: C**. Given the expansion of the definition of "Disabled" under the amended Americans with Disabilities Act ("ADA"), issues arising under it and the FMLA will intersect more than ever. The Equal Employment Opportunity Commission ("EEOC"), as have many courts, has asserted that a request for additional leave might constitute a reasonable accommodation under the ADA. Consequently, in this scenario, the employer should at least engage in the interactive process to determine whether additional leave is possible.

4. If an employer asks a part-time, hourly employee to work on the weekend, the employer must pay that employee:

   a. The employee's regular rate because the Fair Labor Standards Act does not apply to part-time employees.

   b. Time and one-half because weekends and nights require overtime compensation.

   c. The employee's regular rate of pay, unless the weekend work will push the employee over 40 hours of work during that work week.

**ANSWER: C**. As a general matter, the FLSA certainly applies to part-time employees, but it does not include a "nights and weekends" provision, despite the protestations of teenagers everywhere. Time worked on a weekend, with possible exceptions arising under the terms of a collective bargaining agreement or other unique circumstances, is treated as any other "hours worked" under the FLSA. Consequently, any hours worked up to and including the 40-hour threshold, regardless of whether they were worked at night or on a weekend, should be compensated at straight time. Any hours worked over the 40-hour threshold, again regardless of when they were worked, must be compensated as overtime, which is typically 1.5 times and employee's regular hourly wage. It should be noted, however, that the FLSA sets a floor of protection, not a ceiling, and state wage and hour laws must always be consulted as part of this analysis.

5. An employee with a history of reporting late to work has come to your office and reported that her supervisor has repeatedly asked her out for dates despite the fact that she has always declined and told him to stop asking. An hour later, the employee's supervisor stops by your office and informs you that the employee was 20 minutes late for her shift. You should:

    a. Do nothing because it is clear that the employee and the supervisor just don't like each other.

    b. Treat both issues independently, *i.e.* investigate the harassment claim and discipline the employee in accordance with the company's tardiness policy.

    c. Investigate the harassment claim, but ignore the employee's tardiness because it is just too dangerous to discipline an employee who has made a complaint of sexual harassment.

**ANSWER: B**. As a general matter, complaints of harassment should be investigated and resolved. At the same time, an employee cannot insulate himself or herself from legitimate discipline by engaging in protected activity, *i.e.* complaining of harassment and/or discrimination. Consequently, here, the employer should treat the two issues independently. That said, if the employer has generally ignored the employee's tardiness in the past, suddenly choosing to focus on the issue after she has raised a complaint of harassment could place the employer in dangerous territory, but that is a consideration relevant to discipline, and does not impact whether the matter should be addressed at all.

6. An employee has reported that he suffers from migraine headaches, and has sought intermittent leave under the Family and Medical Leave Act. He has a history of taking his sick days on Mondays or Fridays, and often fails to follow company policy regarding the need to call in to report an absence. You should:

   a. Deny the request because, in your opinion, the employee is clearly faking.

   b. Grant the request because the FMLA allows for intermittent leave.

   c. Obtain a medical certification from the employee's medical provider in order to evaluate the request and remind the employee of his obligation to properly report absences.

**ANSWER:** C. Admittedly, the employee in this case looks like a faker, and option A might be tempting, but resist that temptation. Even a heartfelt belief that an employee is lying does not entitle an employer to ignore its obligations under the FMLA. Additionally, while the FMLA does allow for intermittent leave, and migraine headaches generally constitute a qualifying medical condition, employers should not put the cart before the horse. Require employees seeking leave to establish a legitimate basis for the leave through certification from a medical provider. Further, even when employees provide sufficient certification, that does not entitle them to ignore call-in policies and other legitimate workplace rules. Consequently, the best way to curb FMLA abuse is to require employees to adhere to their obligations under the law.

7. Your company is a network provider for TRICARE, pharmacy services and/or medical equipment, and you have just been asked whether the company could be considered a federal subcontractor with affirmative action obligations?

   a. No, the Office of Federal Contract Compliance Program ("OFCCP") has acknowledged that the National Defense Authorization Act of 2012 ("NDAA") excluded TRICARE network providers from the jurisdiction of the OFCCP.

b. Yes, if the company with whom my business has a contract to be a network provider is creating such network as a prime federal contractor.

c. Yes, according to the OFCCP if the only basis of coverage is TRICARE.

d. B and C.

**ANSWER: D**. Affirmative action obligations extend to employers who are subcontractors of prime federal contractors. Subcontractors include network providers of prime federal contractors. The NDAA, which was signed into law in December 2011, exempted TRICARE contracts from the OFCCP's jurisdiction. The OFCCP continues to pursue litigation on the TRICARE issue in OFCCP v. Florida Hospital of Orlando. In July 2013, the Administrative Review Board ("ARB") reconsidered and reversed dismissal of the OFCCP's complaint against Florida Hospital for lack of jurisdiction. Specifically, the ARB found that the NDAA only exempted TRICARE from the OFCCP's jurisdiction under one of the two prongs of the subcontractor definition. Despite finding the OFCCP has jurisdiction over Florida Hospital on the basis of its TRICARE contract, the ARB remanded the case for consideration of whether TRICARE is an exempt federal financial assistance program like Medicare Part A (health insurance) and Part B (Hospital Insurance). We continue to monitor this litigation.

8. The Company hired a new HR director two weeks ago. During the intake process of completing the I-9 form for his first new hire, the COO receives an urgent call from the director. He has discovered that there are I-9 forms only for employees hired in the last year; all others for the nearly 1000 employees are missing. The Company has no foreign national employees so it:

   a. Can tell the HR director to complete, as best as he can, I-9s for those employees without one, leaving blank the sections he can't complete, and put them in a file, saying nothing to the employees.

   b. Do nothing, relying on a five year statute of limitations defense to the potential fines and penalties (which the HR director read about in an HR publication), if ever needed in a federal investigation.

c. Immediately notify all current employees, and those who have left employment if possible, that as a result of a self-audit, HR will need to review their documents from the official list; complete new I-9s with the original hire date, the actual completion date, the employee's signature and a brief explanation.

**ANSWER:** **C**. In this situation, the issue is one of a defective I-9, not a timeliness of completion issue. An I-9 retention (defective) issue is considered by the Department of Labor to be a continuing paperwork violation, unlike that of a timeliness completion issue. Defective I-9s are in violation until they are corrected, so any statute of limitation ("SOL") is tolled throughout the entire period until the correction is made. Consequently, there is no five year SOL available for defective I-9s. Timely completion issues are not continuing violation issues, but the few cases permitting a SOL defense in those circumstances are nearly 20 years old. In today's climate, it is hard to predict whether an SOL defense would even be available in that circumstance.

9. Every year, one of your major customers holds its annual New Year's Eve party at an out of town resort. Employees are not required to attend, but you "highly recommended" that your sales employees attend the party. You pay for a block of rooms at the resort so employees won't be tempted to drive home drunk. A sales employee over-indulges during the festivities and, unfortunately, is found dead in his hotel room the next morning. The coroner rules death by asphyxiation and acute alcohol intoxication. Do you have to report the death to the Occupational Safety and Health Commission ("OSHA")?

a. Yes. OSHA requires that an employer report a fatality from a work-related incident within 8 hours.

b. No. The fatality is not reportable because the fatality is not work-related as the employer did not require attendance at the customer's New Year's Eve party.

c. No. Even though the death may have occurred in the work environment—as attendance was "highly recommended"—the fatality is not reportable as it solely resulted from the employee drinking alcohol for his personal consumption.

**ANSWER: C**. The death does not have to reported to OSHA. In deciding whether an injury, including one resulting in death, is reportable, the employer must determine if the injury is work-related. OSHA presumes that an injury is work-related if it results from events or exposures occurring in the work environment, unless an exception under 29 CFR 1904.5(b)(2) applies. The work environment not only includes the place of business but also any location where "one or more employees are working or are present as a condition of their employment." 29 CFR 1904.5(b)(1). Here, because the employer "highly recommended" attendance at the customer function, the argument could be made that attendance was considered a "condition of employment" and, therefore, the death occurred in the work environment. However, reporting is excused because of the exception provided under 29 CFR 1904.5(b)(2)(iv), as the death was "solely the result of an employee eating, drinking, or preparing food or drink for personal consumption."

10. Your superintendent of manufacturing rushes into your office and tells you that he was accidentally copied on an internal email from an employee, who was soliciting other coworkers to meet a Union organizer for beers after work. Although the employee handbook prohibits personal emails from being sent and received on the employer's internal email system, the policy never has been enforced. Fearing what Union representation would do to your bottom line, you should:

a. Discipline the employee for violating an express handbook policy.

b. Not discipline the employee for this violation, but issue a memorandum a) reminding all employees of the policy and b) your intention to enforce it starting the first of the month.

c. Go to the meeting, buy the first round for all attendees, and listen to why a Union is necessary at your workplace.

<u>**ANSWER:**</u> **B**. While it is true that under current Board precedent, an employer may prohibit the use of its e-mail system for personal e-mail (*see Register-Guard*), the current Board, or at least its General Counsel, does not agree with that position. In fact, at a recent presentation to the Cornell School of Industrial Relations, the General Counsel commented "if the appropriate facts present themselves, I would be urging the Board to revisit *Register-Guard.*" Consequently, an unfair labor practice charge from the terminated employee could pique the Board's interest, which no one wants. Additionally, the fact that the policy has not been previously enforced opens the door for the employee to effectively argue that he was retaliated against for engaging in protected activity. C also is wrong. While it might sound tempting to roll up your sleeves and get to the bottom of the issue over a few pints, doing so would likely be held to constitute unlawful surveillance and/or other interference with your employees' protected concerted activity, all in violation of the NLRA. Consequently, B represents the soundest option under these facts.

*December 2013*

*<u>About the authors and firm</u>

Polsinelli is a first generation law firm serving corporations, institutions, entrepreneurs and individuals nationally. Our attorneys successfully build enduring client relationships by providing practical legal counsel infused with business insight, and with a passion for understanding how to achieve General Counsels' and CEOs' objectives. Polsinelli attorneys invest in understanding their clients' businesses from all angles, as well as the risks, challenges and issues affecting their industry. Ranked 18th in number of U.S. partners* and with more than 700 attorneys in 18 offices from Los Angeles to New York, Polsinelli's organic growth has been driven by the addition of attorneys from top national top law firms. Polsinelli was profiled in the June 2013 issue of *The American Lawyer* as the fastest-growing, full-service law firm in America over a five-year period. The firm's strategic focus is in six areas: healthcare, financial services, real estate, life sciences and technology, energy and business litigation. More broadly, the firm has depth of experience in practices organized around more than 100 services and 70 industries. <u>For more information contact</u>: Scott M. Gilbert, Shareholder, 312.463.6375, sgilbert@polsinelli.com. http://www.polsinelli.com/.

*Polsinelli PC provides this material for informational purposes only.*

*The material provided herein is general and is not intended to be legal advice. Nothing herein should be relied upon or used without consulting a lawyer to consider your specific circumstances, possible changes to applicable laws, rules and regulations and other legal issues. Receipt of this material does not establish an attorney-client relationship. Polsinelli is very proud of the results we obtain for our clients, but you should know that past results do not guarantee future results; that every case is different and must be judged on its own merits; and that the choice of a lawyer is an important decision and should not be based solely upon advertisements.*

# II. BROAD COVERAGE

# Chapter 2

# An Employer's "Top 5" Action Items for 2014

by Frank C. Morris, Jr.*

It's December, and human resources professionals and law departments are reflecting on the issues addressed in 2013 and giving thanks for incident-free holiday parties. But the big question is this: What issues should get priority attention for 2014 as part of a proactive approach to workplace issues and limiting potential employment and labor law claims? This article provides a "Top 5" list of action items to maximize the use of your time and resources for optimum results in 2014.

## 1. Consider Whether Your Organization Should Adopt Mandatory Arbitration Agreements and Seek to Bar Class/Collective Actions in 2014

Over recent years, employer use of mandatory arbitration clauses coupled with class action waivers has been a recurring topic in the courts, before the National Labor Relations Board ("NLRB"), and in Congress. In a series of decisions, including *CompuCredit Corp. v. Greenwood*, *Nitro Lift v. Howard*, *American Express v. Italian Colors Restaurants*, and *AT&T Mobility LLC v. Concepcion*, the U.S. Supreme Court generally endorsed agreements in various contexts that require the use of arbitration, versus resorting to the courts, as the exclusive forum for the resolution of disputes (including statutory claims) under an agreement. And, in *American Express*, the Supreme Court enforced an arbitration agreement that included a class action waiver, relying on the Federal Arbitration Act ("FAA") despite the fact that the costs of an individual arbitration would likely exceed any potential individual recovery.

On the other side of the fence, in 2012, the NLRB ruled in *D.R. Horton* that employer mandatory arbitration agreements with class action waivers allegedly chill employees' right to engage in protected concerted activity under Section 7 of the National Labor Relations Act ("NLRA") and thus are impermissible. D.R. Horton appealed that decision to the U.S. Court of Appeals for the Fifth Circuit. In a 2-1 decision issued on December 3, 2013, the Fifth Circuit reversed the NLRB's ruling and found that the NLRB had failed to give proper weight to the FAA, which generally sanctions the use of arbitration. The Fifth Circuit did, however, agree with the NLRB on a technical but important point, namely that arbitration agreements cannot bar employees from filing charges with the NLRB. The NLRB has not yet indicated whether it will seek Supreme Court review of *D.R. Horton* or choose to litigate the issue in other circuits and hope for a different result.

While the legal landscape is not completely free of doubt in other circuits as to whether mandatory arbitration agreements with class action waivers are permissible, employers may now choose to consider carefully whether such agreements make sense for their particular situations. Note, however, that certain employers may not require mandatory pre-dispute arbitration agreements because of legislation affecting particular businesses. Thus, certain financial services firms are barred under the Dodd-Frank Wall Street Reform and Consumer Protection Act from requiring employees to sign such agreements. Similarly, the Franken Amendment to the Fiscal Year 2010 Department of Defense Appropriations Act bars certain defense contractors from requiring such agreements as to Title VII of the Civil Rights Act of 1964 and certain tort claims.

For the majority of employers that are not barred from requiring employees to execute mandatory pre-dispute arbitration clauses and class/collective action waivers, here are some key pros and cons to consider:

**Potential Pros**

- Potential barring of class actions for wage hour, discrimination, and other labor and employment claims, thereby significantly reducing potential exposure
- Generally a more expeditious resolution of employment claims
- Likely reduced costs for litigation, including discovery

- Less adverse publicity due to a lack of public record court filings and generally private arbitral hearings with decisions only published by consent

- Reduced claims as plaintiffs' attorneys have less incentive to file when class/collective claims are not available

- Ability to couple a mandatory arbitration procedure with a prior mediation requirement

- Lesser risks of a runaway jury verdict

- Limited grounds for judicial review (a pro or a con depending on the arbitrator's ruling)

**Potential Cons**

- There is litigation uncertainty as *D.R. Horton* is binding only in the Fifth Circuit (although several other courts including the Second Circuit in *Sutherland v. Ernst & Young LLP*, also have rejected the NLRB's *D.R. Horton* decision).

- Arbitration can be costly as arbitrators are paid by the employer, and there may be forum fees.

- Arbitrators may be less likely to grant a dispositive legal motion or to enforce procedural rules.

- Arbitrators will generally permit more hearsay and not limit cases as a judge might.

- Arbitrators may have a tendency to try to "split the baby."

- Employees may pursue some claims because employers generally cannot require employees to pay more for an arbitration than the equivalent of court filing fees.

- There are limited grounds for court review, as the Supreme Court held in June 2013 in *Oxford Health Plans v. Sutter*.

- Drafting and implementing an arbitration and/or dispute resolution program and class action waivers must be carefully done to avoid various potential pitfalls (including barring the filing of NLRB charges).

In short, the new year and new legal developments may make this an apt time to consider whether a mandatory arbitration/mediation program and class/collective action waivers would make sense for your organization.

**2. Enhance the Accessibility of Your Organization's Website to Individuals with Disabilities**

Virtually all for-profit and not-for-profit entities rely on their website as a key adjunct for their business activities and customer or client transactions. It is therefore not surprising that litigation may result if such websites are not accessible to individuals with disabilities, such as vision or hearing impairments. This point was forcefully driven home on November 25, 2013, when the Civil Rights Division of the U.S. Department of Justice ("DOJ") intervened in a lawsuit against H&R Block's Tax Preparation website that was originally filed by the National Federation of the Blind and other plaintiffs.

Title III of the Americans with Disabilities Act ("ADA") provides that a public accommodation—which would include most businesses and nonprofits—may not prevent individuals with disabilities from "the opportunity . . . to participate in or benefit from the goods, services, facilities, privileges, advantages or accommodations" of a covered entity. Discrimination includes a "failure to make reasonable modifications in policies, practices or procedures, when such modifications are necessary to afford such goods, services, facilities, privileges, advantages or accommodations to individuals with disabilities."

The DOJ's press release in the H&R Block website case notes that "many individuals with disabilities," including individuals "who are blind, deaf or have physical disabilities with an impact on manual dexterity, use computers and the Internet with the help of assistive technologies." DOJ points to such technologies as screen reader software, which makes audible information otherwise presented on a computer screen; captioning, which translates video narration and sound into text; and keyboard navigation rather than mouse-based navigation for individuals with visual, hearing, or manual dexterity disabilities. Such technologies are reflected in guidelines called the Web Content Accessibility Guidelines ("WCAG") 2.0 for making website content accessible to individuals with disabilities.

DOJ says that its participation in this lawsuit, like others, is warranted because, as noted in the press release, inaccessible websites "deny persons with disabilities access to basic goods and services that people without disabilities take advantage of every day." Vigorous advocacy groups for the disabled have also pursued lawsuits challenging allegedly inaccessible websites for appointment scheduling, health care records, treatment follow-up, the purchase of goods and services, and other purposes. DOJ has also promulgated an Advance Notice of Proposed Rulemaking to implement Titles II and III of the ADA to establish requirements for making goods and services "offered by public accommodations via the Internet, specifically at sites on the World Wide Web (Web) accessible to individuals with disabilities."

Thus, prudent businesses should consider taking steps in 2014 to enhance the accessibility of their websites to individuals with disabilities to avoid both litigation and adverse publicity.

### 3. Ensure That Proper Exempt/Nonexempt and Independent Contractor/Employee Determinations and Updated Job Descriptions Are in Place in 2014

Never has the potential peril for misclassification of individuals as independent contractors or employees as exempt been greater. As each level of government tries to ferret out every possible dollar of potential tax revenue, a target of choice has become the alleged employer misclassification of individuals as independent contractors because of the reduced payroll taxes from independent contractors versus employees. Employer problems in this area are compounded by differences between the Internal Revenue Service ("IRS"), U.S. Department of Labor ("DOL"), and Equal Employment Opportunity Commission tests for independent contractors' status. The plaintiffs' bar in recent years has pursued class and collective misclassification claims under the Fair Labor Standards Act ("FLSA") and state and local wage hour laws as proverbial pots of gold. The potential stakes will rise in 2014 as many jurisdictions raise their minimum wages well above the federal FLSA $7.25 per hour level. For example, Montgomery and Prince George's counties in Maryland are going to $11.50 per hour, and Washington, D.C., and California are significantly raising their levels. Voters in a referendum raised the minimum wage in an area around the Seattle-Tacoma International Airport to $15 per hour. And, of course, there is a national campaign focused on fast food restaurants to raise the minimum wage to $15 per hour.

A new threat to employers from misclassification arises from the Affordable Care Act ("ACA"). An individual misclassified as an independent contractor could bring a claim against, as well as trigger an ACA penalty for, an employer not offering essential health care coverage if the person was ultimately held to be an employee. The penalty for failure to provide minimum essential health benefits is equal to the number of full-time employees times $166.66 *per month* for every employee after the first 30 employees. Any termination of the "contractor" after such a claim of misclassification could also trigger a retaliation claim under the ACA's broad retaliation provision, Section 1558. The IRS and DOL have advised that a focus of their audit and enforcement activities will be to identify misclassified workers. Thus, this aspect of the ACA adds to the already broad tax and wage hour exposure for the misclassification of employees as independent contractors.

In addition, it is also being argued that if an applicable large employer fails to offer coverage to individuals who are held to be employees rather than contractors, they may be liable for the medical claims of those individuals who did not have coverage. If this position is adopted, an employer could face massive bills if such an individual has, for example, a catastrophic accident or serious illness.

The burgeoning number of disability discrimination claims since the enactment of the American with Disabilities Amendments Act is also relevant. Just as a job description may be critical evidence in proving that an employee was properly classified as exempt, it may also be critical evidence in showing the essential functions of a job and helping to establish whether an employee or applicant could perform them.

In light of the potential wage hour, tax, ACA, and ADA exposure, one potential high-priority objective for human resources leadership in 2014 is to undertake a review of current independent contractors and to make sure that such individuals actually fit the multi-factor test to qualify as independent contractors. This process should include a review of key contractual provisions that support independent contractor status as well as those to avoid as inconsistent with independent contractor status.

Similarly, to the extent there are employees classified as exempt, where there may be questions as to the propriety of that classification, a new year review of whether such employees actually fit within the executive, administrative, professional, outside sales, computer professional, or other FLSA exemptions is well warranted. Part of that review should involve assessing whether a position's job description reflects duties that qualify for an exemption and, when appropriate, revising the description or the classification. In addition, assuring that the essential functions of the position, including items like attendance and ability to communicate, when appropriate, are documented in the job description is necessary. This effort can mean the difference between success and failure on a disability claim, especially an intellectual disability claim. A strategic point is that performing a review of classification issues and revisions of job descriptions under the direction of counsel for the purpose of seeking and providing legal advice will create the best basis for assertion of the attorney-client privilege to documents created in the review process.

### 4. Update Confidentiality and Non-Compete Agreements to Better Protect Intellectual Property and Human Capital Assets in a High-Technology, BYOD, Mobile World

As we approach 2014, employers increasingly face employees who seek to go to work for competitors or to start their own similar business. Given the proliferation of employers utilizing BYOD (Bring Your Own Device) policies, the ubiquitous presence of high-resolution cameras on smartphones and flash drives and other small memory devices, questions abound as to how to protect an organization's commercially valuable information and prevent unfair competition in this ever-evolving high-tech world. Conceptually, the answers are the same as before: confidentiality, non-compete, and non-solicitation agreements. But, to be effective in 2014, these can't be the agreements of your grandparents or even your parents. They must be adapted to both evolving legal standards and changing technology to provide enforceable protections.

Non-compete and confidentiality agreements are employment agreements that will be governed by the vagaries of state laws. This means the first principle is that a multistate employer needs to draft agreements that will be enforceable in the states where the employer operates, recognizing that one-size agreements really fit no one and offer little protection.

Key points to consider to create enforceable and effective non-competes that will protect your organization from unfair competition in 2014 and beyond, include, among others, the following:

- Length of restriction
    - Different periods depending on type, job, and level of employee
    - Reserving the right to shorten or lengthen within 10 days of the employees' termination
- Scope of restriction
    - Only consistent with legitimate business interests
    - Consistent with the employee's duties for your organization
    - More narrowly tailored, greater likelihood of enforcement
- Geographic scope
    - Only consistent with legitimate business interests
    - Again, consistent with the scope of the employee's duties for your organization
    - Broader the area, harder to enforce

- State law statutory limitations, *e.g.*,
  - Florida Statutes Anno. §542.33 (sets forth presumptively reasonable and unreasonable time periods for various types of restrictions)
  - Oregon Revised Statute §653.295 (limits non-competes based on various factors)
  - California Business and Professional Code §16600 *et seq.* (generally, non-competes and non-solicits of customers are impermissible)
- Tolling period of restrictive covenant during actual or threatened breach
- Assignability of agreements with restrictive covenants
  - Such clauses are usually helpful in sale or merger situations
  - Without them, critical human capital may be lost
- Liquidated damage provisions
  - Do liquidated damage provisions preclude injunctive relief to enforce a restrictive covenant?
- Choice of law provisions
  - Can be critical to securing enforcement
- Choice of forum provisions
  - Can be tactically important
- Waiver of need for bonds in connection with injunctive relief
- Blue penciling
  - Provide that, if a court finds a provision of an agreement overbroad and enforceable, the employer will redraft and the

employee is obligated to consent (this may work in states where the court will not blue pencil).

- o Provide that a court is expressly authorized to "blue pencil" or revise an overbroad provision (only effective in some states).

- Is continued employment sufficient consideration for a non-compete?

- Requiring an accounting of and return of confidential information at termination

Careful attention to these items and related issues will provide employers with non-competes and non-solicits with the best prospects for successful enforcement.

*Confidentiality and Non-Disclosure Agreements*

An employer will have a very hard time justifying a non-compete for low-level employees. But even low-level employees can abscond with an employer's trade secrets or confidential and commercially valuable information, especially given today's technology. The upshot is that potentially all employees may be asked to execute appropriate confidentiality agreements. But as with mandatory arbitration agreements and class action waivers, the NLRB has intruded into this area, even as to union-free employers. In *Flex Frac Logistics* (2012), the NLRB held that an employer may not bar non-manager or supervisory employees from disclosing "company information" if the term can be interpreted to include information regarding employers' wages, discipline, or performance or customer information and "personal information and documents." The NLRB also claims that employer bans on discussing "jobs, company business or work projects" may chill protected concerted activity under the NLRA. An NLRB Administrative Law Judge reached similar conclusions in *Quicken Loans, Inc.* (Jan. 8, 2013). While the courts may well reject the NLRB's holdings in *Flex Frac Logistics* and *Quicken Loans* as the Fifth Circuit did in *D.R. Horton* regarding class action waivers, for now, employers should attempt to draft confidentiality agreements to try and avoid the NLRB problem. Key points to consider in drafting lawful confidentiality agreements include, among others, the following:

- Avoid all-inclusive overbroad language.
    - Don't try to bar all discussions of terms and conditions of employment, including wage and benefits and employee contact information.
- Use appropriate disclaimers and examples in the policy to demonstrate that it is not intended to restrict the exercise of NLRA Section 7 rights.
- Consider including exceptions to clarify what is not covered.
    - For example, communications with third parties such as attorneys, union representatives, tax advisors, and accountants are not covered.
    - Clarify that activity protected by NLRA Section 7, such as discussions of terms and conditions of employment, is not prohibited.
- Be aware that companies may distinguish between supervisors and management and non-management as only the latter is covered by the NLRA.
- Avoid blanket policies against employees criticizing or disparaging the employer or management and instead use carefully-tailored ones.

*Issues Arising in Hiring a Competitor's Employee*

Finally, remember that practical steps can be taken when hiring from a competitor to avoid or minimize potential liability for contractual, common law, and statutory claims. Ask a potential new hire if he/she is bound by restrictive covenants or confidentiality agreements with prior employers. Such commitments might be hidden in option or incentive compensation agreements as well as in standalone agreements. Have an expert review any restrictive covenant of a prospective hire as to the likelihood that it is enforceable. Assess whether the candidate could adhere to any restrictions and still perform the essential functions of the position you might offer. Consider whether it is appropriate for the candidate to seek a waiver of restrictions but understand that this is his/her choice. Evaluate if you could park the candidate "on the bench" with other duties for the duration of the restricted period. Don't imply that you will indemnify the candidate in the event of a legal challenge by the former employer unless you are prepared to do so. And finally, if the employee is to be given an offer, have him/her certify in writing that he/she has not taken or given to your organization any confidential or proprietary information of any prior employer.

Following the above guidance should provide your organization with confidentiality and non-compete agreements that have the greatest likelihood of being enforced while also providing maximum protection against claims by a new employee's former employer. In today's highly competitive world, it is well worth the effort to maximize protection against unfair competition and disclosure of the proprietary business information that gives your organization a commercial advantage or competitive edge—and carefully-tailored agreements can help you do this.

## 5. Consider Key Employer ACA Issues for 2014

As of January 1, 2014, employers should review their compliance with the ever-evolving requirements of the Affordable Care Act (ACA). The well-publicized delay of the "pay or play" employer mandate, while helpful to employers, did not eliminate many compliance issues for employers. Among key issues for employers to consider:

- Create and distribute to employees SBCs (Summaries of Benefits and Coverage) in 2014 using an updated template from the DOL.
- Report minimum value calculations, which are necessary for employer-sponsored health plans for the 2014 plan year, in written notices about the health insurance exchanges (exchanges), which were due by October 1, 2013, as well as in SBCs to be provided during 2014 annual enrollment.

- Confirm if your organization is an applicable large employer.
  - This will include a determination of whether the employees of "related entities" must be counted to determine applicable large employer status under the test in Section 414 of the Internal Revenue Code.
- Reexamine the facts around individuals classified as independent contractors; as noted in item #3 above, both IRS and DOL have made the misclassification issue a focus of their audit and enforcement plans and liabilities for misclassification can be significant.
- Review any leased or temporary employee agreements; entities obtaining workers from temporary and leasing agencies could be found to be co-employers with the agencies, and the consequence would be joint and several liability for ACA penalties as of 2015.
  - Treasury regulations also provide that an applicable large employer is subject to ACA penalties for workers who are deemed to be "common law" employees under IRS tests.
- For insured plans, seek a certification, preferably with an indemnification provision, that a plan your business secures is ACA-compliant for 2014.
- Review employer-sponsored plans.
  - Eliminate pre-existing condition limitations.
  - Eliminate annual caps on essential health benefits.
  - Assure that the plan provides essential health benefits.
  - Ensure that the plan offers coverage for adult children to age 26.
  - Assure that waiting periods don't exceed 90 days.
  - Confirm that out-of-pocket limitations applicable to both insured and self-insured non-grandfathered plans do not exceed

$6,350 for employee-only coverage and $12,700 for family coverage.

    - Assure that 2013 W-2 reporting will provide ACA-required information.

- Consider current steps to avoid January 1, 2018, "Cadillac" tax liability.

    - Remember, on January 1, 2018, a 40-percent non-deductible excise tax will be imposed on plans where the combined employer and employee costs exceed $10,200 for employee-only coverage and $27,500 for family coverage; it is estimated that 60 percent of all large employer plans would already exceed these thresholds even without considering cost increases between now and 2018.

    - Consider taking advantage of the more generous incentives available under ACA Wellness Programs regulations and the potential long-term reductions in health care costs that they can provide while improving the health, attendance, and productivity of employees (but pay close attention to complying with the Wellness regulations).

    - Consider value-based purchasing and securing higher-quality but lower-cost benefit plans or providers.

    - Consider the use of on-site clinics; perhaps set them up with other employers in the area or through industry groups.

- Be cautious not to take adverse action without good justification against any employees who receive a premium subsidy or who complain about implementation of an employer-sponsored plan to avoid claims under the broad retaliation provisions of Section 1558 of the ACA.

Employer attention to these issues is essential to avoid liability under the employer mandate commencing in 2015 and to prevent ACA whistleblower claims in 2014 and beyond. The plethora of ACA regulations that will continue to be issued by the Treasury Department, IRS, and DOL will add new challenges to employer compliance with the ACA in 2014. Finally, now is the time to take actions to avoid the Cadillac tax in 2018.

*December 2013*

*About the author and firm

Frank C. Morris, Jr., fmorris@ebglaw.com, (202) 861-1880, is a Member of Epstein Becker & Green, P.C., in the Firm's Washington, DC office, where he heads the Labor & Employment Practice. He is also Director of the Firm's national Disability Practice Group.

Epstein Becker & Green, P.C., a national law firm, is uncompromising in its pursuit of legal excellence and client service in its areas of practice: Health Care and Life Sciences, Labor and Employment, Litigation, Corporate Services, and Employee Benefits. The firm is proud to be a trusted advisor to clients in the health care and life sciences, financial services, retail and hospitality industries, among others, representing entities from startups to Fortune 100 companies and nonprofits.

*This document has been provided for informational purposes only and is not intended and should not be construed to constitute legal advice. Please consult your attorneys in connection with any fact-specific situation under federal law and the applicable state or local laws that may impose additional obligations on you and your organization.*

# Chapter 3

# A Review of Labor and Employment Policy in 2013: What's Next in 2014?

by Harold P. Coxson*

As 2013 comes to a close, it's time to assess what happened and what didn't happen in Washington, D.C. during the year in terms of labor and employment law legislation, regulations, and litigation. The short version is that Congress remained gridlocked, there was an explosion of new but not finalized regulations, and a number of courts and government agencies issued significant decisions. What can be expected in 2014 and beyond from Congress and the federal agencies? Of course, 2014 is a congressional midterm election year, which will dictate much of the debate in Congress.

## 2013: ANOTHER BAD YEAR FOR CONGRESS

Although the first session of the 113th Congress in 2013 produced the lowest output of legislation in history and Congress received the lowest public approval rating on record, the first session of the two-year congressional cycle ended on a positive note. Congress passed a two-year budget deal that will keep the government running through 2015. As with most legislative compromises, the new budget deal does not please everyone. It maintains a large portion of the indiscriminate, across-the-board sequester cuts in government spending and does not create new government programs. But it also does not raise taxes to restore funding for the programs previously cut by sequester. Depending on one's point of view, that is either good news or bad news.

Some had suggested in lieu of a budget deal that Congress pass a continuing resolution maintaining the status quo including the full sequester budget cuts to domestic spending and the defense budget. They will be disappointed. As will those who demanded a complete roll-back of the sequester.

Instead, passage of the two-year budget compromise eases the pressure created by the threat of another government shutdown, but sets up two key votes by Congress early in 2014: (1) a vote on a comprehensive omnibus appropriations bill on how to allocate the budget throughout the government; and (2) a vote on whether to extend the debt ceiling.

The result of the 2013 budget compromise is a budget of $1.012 trillion in 2014 and $1.014 trillion in 2015, which is a compromise halfway between the president's requested budget and that proposed by the Republican-led House of Representatives. Of course it does not reduce the deficit, which stands at $17.2 trillion. The budget deficit must be extended by next February or March to raise the debt ceiling.

The 2013 budget deal also does not establish how the money is to be divided among the 12 appropriations bills that fund federal government agencies. The congressional appropriations committees are hard at work to fashion new spending limits for each of the 12 bills. The outcome should be determined before the January 15 deadline and perhaps passed by an Omnibus Spending Bill approved by House and Senate Appropriations Committees.

Also, Congress adjourned for 2013 without extending long-term unemployment benefits, which means that unemployment benefits for the long-term unemployed will expire on December 31. That sets up another critical fiscal vote early in 2014 soon after Congress returns to start its second session.

## IS PASSAGE OF THE 2013 BUDGET COMPROMISE A TURNING POINT FOR CONGRESS?

Does passage of the budget deal by bipartisan, bicameral compromise signed by the president portend passage of other legislation by compromise in 2014 during the next session of Congress? Probably not—at least not on the labor and employment law battlefields. One possible exception remains some form of immigration legislation, most likely to be piecemeal reforms rather than a grand comprehensive bill, including a path to legal status (or "amnesty"), which passed the Senate in 2013. Perhaps

Congress also will vote on a much-needed reform of the endangered and badly-underfunded multi-employer pension system with its legacy withdrawal liability, which exceeds many companies' entire net worth and threatens their very survival. Something should also be done to replace and improve the current Pension Protection Act of 2006, which sunsets at the end of 2014.

There may be a few other election-year votes in 2014 as well, such as one on a minimum wage increase but without indexation of automatic future increases and another on the Employment Non-Discrimination Act (ENDA) to address employment discrimination on the basis of sexual orientation, sexual preference, or gender identity, which passed the Senate in 2013.

But, in general, employers should not expect that passage of the budget deal will bring about a new era of comity between the two political parties or the two legislative bodies in 2014. Until the results of the 2014 elections are in, and possibly even thereafter, employers should not expect bipartisanship in Congress, especially not on the labor and employment agenda.

## THE ABYSMAL RECORD OF THE FIRST SESSION OF THE 113TH CONGRESS

Congress passed only 59 bills in 2013, which is a very small fraction of the 6,366 bills introduced during the first session of the 113th Congress. That figure represents the lowest one-year output in congressional history, lower even than what President Truman described as the "do-nothing Congress" of 1947-48, which passed only 395 bills during the first session of the 80th Congress and 511 during the second session. The 2013 record low is a sharp decline even from 2011 and 2012 when Congress passed 90 and 148 bills respectively, and it's a big drop from the 258 bills passed in 2010.

Again, depending on one's point of view, the sluggish rate of passage of new legislation is either good news or bad news. It's good news, of course, if bills you oppose such as the Employee Free Choice Act (EFCA or "card check" bill) are not passed, but it's bad news if bills you may support, such as modification of the Affordable Care Act (ACA or

Obamacare) are not passed either. The House passed 40 bills attempting to repeal or modify Obamacare, but the Senate passed none.

In assessing the record of Congress in 2013, as the old saying goes, "where you sit depends upon where you stand." According to Gallup polls, however, the public's job approval rating for Congress in 2013 averaged only 14 percent—the lowest in Gallup's history. Certainly not a poll any incumbent from any party would welcome going into an election year.

## 2013: A BAD YEAR FOR GOVERNMENT AGENCIES

In 2013 there was a prolonged government shutdown during which many government workers were humbled to find out that they were "nonessential" and furloughed. Yet the record of accomplishment in 2013 was not that impressive in any event, despite a flood of proposed but not finally implemented new regulations with administrative policies and decisions still pending review in the federal courts.

After the ACA's high water mark in June of 2012 when the Supreme Court of the United States declared that it was constitutional, it was all downhill. In July of 2013, the U.S. Treasury Department delayed implementation of the law's employer "play or pay" mandate until 2015 because the law was not ready for implementation. In October, that lack of preparation was demonstrated when hundreds of people were unable to enroll due to glitches with the federal health insurance website. Next, the biggest blow came in December when it was confirmed that millions of policy holders were informed by their insurance companies that their existing health plans were being cancelled because the plans did not conform to the ACA—belying the president's unequivocal assurance throughout passage of the act that no one would lose coverage of their health plans. A November 17 *The Wall Street Journal* editorial projected the bad news: "Millions of Americans are losing their plans and paying more for health care, and doctors are being forced out of insurance networks."

Obamacare is still the law with an effective date of January 1, 2014, for provisions not delayed or deferred, but implementation will move forward in 2014 under continuing attack. Even organized labor, originally a strong proponent of the ACA, threatened to support repeal unless labor's demands were met. The Obama administration issued a proposed rule to exempt, starting in 2015, union-controlled health insurance plans (commonly referred to as Taft-Hartley plans) from the ACA's reinsurance tax on self-insured health-care plans. If union plans were carved out, the result would advantage union organizing in companies that must pay the reinsurance tax on self-insured plans. Watch for this to be a major labor-management issue in 2014.

## WHAT'S AHEAD FOR LABOR AND EMPLOYMENT LAW ISSUES IN 2014?

One result of congressional inaction is that it shifts focus to the federal regulators and regulatory agencies such as the U.S. Department of Labor's Occupational Safety and Health Administration (OSHA), Wage and Hour Division (WHD), and Office of Federal Contract Compliance Programs (OFCCP), the National Labor Relations Board (NLRB), and the U.S. Equal Employment Opportunity Commission (EEOC). The government's record of new and proposed regulations, expanded enforcement through regulatory and sub-regulatory policies, and overturning of long-established legal precedent through administrative case law decisions over the past several years stands in dramatic contrast to Congressional inaction. Expect that trend to continue in 2014.

For example, among the regulatory actions in 2013 by federal executive branch agencies, the OFCCP issued proposed regulations requiring federal contractors to advance hiring and employment "goals" for veterans and the disabled. The WHD continued work on its "right to know" regulation, which will require employers to justify overtime exempt classifications, including independent contractor status, through notification to employees of the basis for their classifications. In sub-regulatory action, OSHA issued an interpretive letter approving walk around rights of outside union organizers to accompany OSHA inspectors during workplace safety and health investigations. Among independent federal agencies, the EEOC issued rules limiting the use of criminal background checks and credit references in hiring.

Also, near the end of the year there even was renewed discussion in Washington of stricter rules governing federal contracting by companies with wage and hour and safety and health violations as a result of a new report released by Senate Health, Education, Labor and Pensions (HELP) Committee Chairman Tom Harkin. That discussion is reminiscent of the "high road" proposal led by Vice President Biden early in the administration and the ill-fated "government contractor blacklisting" regulation proposed by the Clinton administration. The latter, which would have revised the Federal Acquisition Regulation (FAR) to deny federal contractors the eligibility to bid on federal contracts based on their compliance with labor and employment laws, went through the full rulemaking process and was issued as a "midnight regulation" in the closing days of the administration. The rule was rescinded at the start of the Bush administration.

Ironically, one of the biggest developments in the 2013 Congress was the Senate's procedural rule change based on a simple majority vote (the "nuclear option"), which strengthens the regulatory hammerlock by eliminating the 60-vote filibuster on executive branch appointments and judicial nominations. Trying to avoid the nuclear option, the Senate agreed to confirm all five candidates to the NLRB and its General Counsel, resulting in a pro-union majority for the foreseeable future. The Senate also confirmed Secretary of Labor Thomas Perez and is in the process of confirming three new judicial appointments to the D.C. Circuit Court of Appeals, which will result in tilting the balance on what many consider to be the second most important federal court after the Supreme Court of the United States. These newly-confirmed appointments assure a liberal, pro-union agenda in federal agencies such as the NLRB and greater difficulty in successfully challenging agency regulations and administrative case decisions in the D.C. Circuit for years to come.

## ADMINISTRATION REGULATORY PRIORITIES

Defense and implementation of the beleaguered ACA will be the administration's top priority in 2014. So it's unlikely that the White House will welcome other major new regulatory fights to distract attention from the ACA, especially in an election year. Nevertheless, regulatory battles begun in 2013 and before may not simply be abandoned in 2014. Certainly, organized labor will pressure for their advance. Here are only a few of the potential regulatory issues to watch for next year.

1. Revisions to the LMRDA "Persuader Activity" Regulations

The administration's most far-reaching sop to organized labor is its proposed revisions to the "persuader activity" reporting requirements. The Department of Labor intends to publish a final rule in March 2014 revising its interpretation of the "advice exemption" under section 203(c) of the Labor-Management Reporting and Disclosure Act of 1959 (LMRDA) that currently exempts legal advice from public disclosure and reporting requirements that apply to employers and other persons in connection with efforts to persuade employees concerning union organizing, collective bargaining, strikes, and other forms of concerted activity. Reporting by employers and outside consultants and law firms is required when a "persuader" is hired to communicate directly with employees regarding unionization. But for over 50 years the law has exempted "advice"—especially legal advice—from the reporting requirement.

The revised interpretation under the proposed persuader rule would narrow dramatically, if not entirely eviscerate, the scope of the advice exemption by requiring consultants, management-side labor law firms, public relations firms, and trade associations to report activities broadly defined in the proposed regulation as "persuader" services. That would include common labor relations services designed to prevent unfair labor practices, such as review, preparation, and provision of speeches, written and electronic materials, and supervisory training, including seminars and workshops.

In particular, lawyers and law firms, and their corporate clients, will be pressured to disclose attorney-client confidences. In dealing with that pressure, they will have to decide whether to disclose this confidential information (thus potentially violating Rule 1.6 of the American Bar Association (ABA) Model Rules of Professional Conduct, which was made binding under state bar association rules, and thereby potentially subjecting themselves to discipline, including disbarment) or protecting the confidences by not reporting, which would arguably subject them to civil and criminal penalties, including imprisonment, under the LMRDA.

The DOL is also likely to argue that under the proposed regulation, lawyers and law firms must report all "labor relations advice and services" for all clients, even those for whom the lawyer provides no persuader work, whenever the lawyer reports such services for a single client. According to ABA comments filed during the rulemaking that demanded withdrawal of the proposed rule, the reporting requirement would unjustifiably interfere with employer access to counsel by making it difficult for businesses that do not have in-house legal and labor relations expertise—especially small businesses—from retaining outside legal counsel during union organizing and collective bargaining. That, in turn, would conflict with the National Labor Relations Act's employer "free speech" rights in union representation elections and could lead to "back door" EFCA-like forced card check recognition and bargaining where uncounseled employers commit serious unfair labor practices. The intended result is to reverse the steady decline in private sector union density by making it more difficult for employers to communicate lawfully with their employees during a union organizing campaign and collective bargaining. A more in depth discussion of the persuader regulation proposal is available in our article, "Labor Agencies Double-Team Business Community with Onerous Rules."

2. NLRB "Ambush Election" Rules for Union Representation Elections

2013 was a bad year for the NLRB. The Supreme Court is reviewing the decision of the D.C. Circuit Court of Appeals in *Noel Canning v. NLRB* holding that the recess appointments to the agency on January 4, 2012, were unconstitutional and that thereafter the agency's decisions and other actions were invalid for lack of a quorum. The case will be argued to the Supreme Court in January and a decision thereafter may necessitate the NLRB to reconsider hundreds of previously-issued decisions.

As a result of the uncertainty, the pace of reversals of long-established precedent by the recess-appointed Board slowed noticeably in 2013. However, now with a new, fully-confirmed five-member Board and General Counsel expect the pace of decisions and regulations to pick up in 2014 with a pro-union majority. One pending issue of overriding importance is union organizing on a company's email system at work and other forms of electronic equipment. Watch for the long-awaited Board decision in *Roundy's Inc.* to serve as the vehicle for an exception to a company's "no solicitation" policy.

One of the casualties of the D.C. Circuit decision was the NLRB's dramatic overhaul of its union representation election rules (the so-called "ambush election" or "quickie election" rules), which would dramatically shorten the time between when a union files an election petition—presumably at its peak of support among the proposed unit of employees—and the actual date of the election. The rule would have resulted in most union representation elections occurring within two weeks of the union's petition by eliminating pre-election litigation to determine such critical issues as voter eligibility and the composition of the bargaining unit.

The rule was challenged in the D.C. Circuit and thereafter held in abeyance pending the Supreme Court's review of the *Noel Canning* case as to whether the NLRB had the authority to act. Finally, in December the NLRB threw in the towel on its appeal in support of the representation election rules and withdrew the appeal but is expected to reissue an even stronger version of the rules in 2014.

In 2013, the NLRB also lost several high-profile appeals court decisions; in at least two of these cases, Ogletree Deakins represented the prevailing employers. The first was a successful challenge by the Chamber of Commerce of the United States and the South Carolina Chamber of Commerce to the NLRB's "notice posting" rule. In *Chamber of Commerce of the United States v. NLRB*, the Fourth Circuit Court of Appeals struck down the rule, which mandated that all private sector employers post a workplace notice informing employees of their right to join or form a union. Both the Fourth Circuit and the D.C. Circuit in a separate case held that the rule exceeded the agency's authority under the National Labor Relations Act and violated employers' free speech rights to remain silent.

In the second case, *D.R. Horton, Inc. v. NLRB*, which was also argued by Ogletree Deakins, the Fifth Circuit Court of Appeals upheld the employer's argument in favor of class action waivers in mandatory employment law arbitration agreements. The NLRB had ruled that such waivers violated employees' rights to engage in protected concerted activity. In denying enforcement of the Board's order, the Fifth Circuit held that under the authority of the Federal Arbitration Act and several Supreme Court decisions employers could insist on class action waivers in arbitration agreements.

However, the NLRB did prevail before the Sixth Circuit Court of Appeals in *Specialty Healthcare*, which upheld the Board's decision approving micro-sized, fragmented, single job description bargaining units over an employer's objection for a broader, more inclusive unit—unless the employer could prove the difficult standard that the excluded employees shared an "overwhelming" community of interests with employees in the union's petitioned-for unit. That standard will continue to be problematic for employers.

3. OSHA "Injury and Illness Prevention Program" (I2P2)

OSHA is developing a rule requiring employers to identify hazards in the workplace and then implement an Injury and Illness Prevention Program to address them. It involves planning, implementing, evaluating, and improving processes and activities designed to protect employee safety and health that would be monitored by employees and enforceable by OSHA even without an established standard. The proposed rule would require employers to develop safety and health plans with their employees that would become enforceable even in lieu of a specific OSHA safety and health standard. For that reason, the proposal is considered a "back door ergonomics standard," which was rejected by Congress pursuant to the Congressional Review Act nearly a decade ago. The target date for promulgation of the I2P2 rule is September 2014.

4. U.S. Equal Employment Opportunity Commission (EEOC)

Not to be outdone, EEOC also has an aggressive agenda of investigation and enforcement policies. EEOC's Regulatory Agenda includes several "priorities" for Fiscal Years 2013-2016 which bear watching. Among those priorities are:

- Eliminating systemic barriers in recruitment and hiring
- Immigrant, migrant, and other vulnerable workers
- Emerging issues: ADA Amendments Act; Lesbian, Gay, Bisexual, and Transgender issues; pregnancy and forced unpaid leave
- Compensation & gender discrimination
- Access to the legal system—retaliation & releases

- Harassment
- Also, EEOC's Strategic Enforcement Plan includes criminal background checks, in which EEOC has announced it will focus on:
    - Disparate impact discrimination
    - Especially involving charges of Race & National Origin discrimination
    - Blanket prohibitions on hiring convicted felons are inherently suspect. (EEOC has pursued employers that have broad prohibitions on hiring applicants with conviction records).

Finally, employers are challenging EEOC's increasingly aggressive investigation and enforcement policies through oversight hearings and proposed legislation in Congress, and legal challenges in the courts to make sure that the Agency fulfills its statutory duty under Title VII to attempt good faith conciliation and mediation prior to initiating an enforcement action. For the most part, courts have agreed with employers on that point with the notable exception of the Seventh Circuit's decision in *EEOC v. Mach Mining* where the court ruled that alleged failure to conciliate is not an affirmative defense to the merits of a discrimination suit. Thus, the Seventh Circuit disagreed with its sister circuits, including the Eighth, Second, Eleventh, Sixth, Fifth, Fourth, and Tenth Circuits, and held that the statutory directive to the EEOC to negotiate first and sue later does not implicitly create a defense for employers who have allegedly violated Title VII. (*EEOC v Mach Mining, LLC*, December 20, 2013). Undoubtedly, Mach Mining will seek Supreme Court review through the filing of a petition for certiorari.

## CONCLUSION

2014 may be slightly more productive in Congress (it could hardly be less productive than 2013), but most of the attention will be directed toward congressional oversight on the implementation of Obamacare and on the 2014 midterm congressional elections where all 435 House seats and 35 Senate seats (21 held by Democrats and 14 held by Republicans) are up for election, as well as states in which incumbent senators have announced retirement. Expect most of the labor and employment agenda in Washington again to be driven by federal agencies and by the reviewing federal courts.

## POSTSCRIPT

Events of the first quarter of 2014 have been consistent with the article's predictions. The NLRB withdrew its highly-controversial final rule on revised procedures for union representation elections (termed by management as the "ambush election" rules), which had been struck down by the U.S. Court of Appeals for the District of Columbia Circuit based on the Board's lack of a three-member quorum required to issue the final rule. The new fully-confirmed five-member Board next reissued a Notice of Proposed Rulemaking (NPRM) for the exact same rules as originally proposed in 2011. The record for the 2014 NPRM includes over 65,000 comments from the original 2011 rulemaking, as well as new written comments submitted this year and the record of a two-day hearing. The record closed on April 14; a final rule is expected well before December when the term of Board Member Nancy Schiffer expires and the remaining Board could potentially be deadlocked two-to-two.

Also, on another hugely controversial issue, the Labor Department announced postponement of its proposed revisions to the LMRDA's "persuader activity" regulations, originally due in March. As drafted, the rule would limit the "advice" exemption for reporting and public disclosure of outside legal advice to employers during union organizing, collective bargaining, and concerted activity. Employers, together with the American Bar Association and state bar associations argue that the rule would force employers to disclose attorney-client confidences in violation of Rule 1.6 of the Model Rules of Professional Responsibility. This would put lawyers in jeopardy of state bar sanctions, including disbarment, for violating attorney confidences through reporting *or* criminal prosecution, including imprisonment, under the Labor-Management Reporting and Disclosure Act for failure to report. Litigation is threatened when the final rule is promulgated. The future outlook for the rule is uncertain.

Finally, other major developments during the first quarter of 2014 included two new presidential Executive Orders on increasing the minimum wage, strengthening pay equity and anti-retaliation rules for employees of federal contractors, and a presidential directive to the

Department of Labor to rewrite the overtime pay rules under Part 541 of the Fair Labor Standards Act regulations for salary-exempt administrative, executive and professional employees. This stems from President Obama's declaration during the January 28 State of the Union that he would act unilaterally and not wait for Congress to act on these and other issues.

In Congress, all eyes are focused on the mounting number of announced retirements among long-term members, and, of course, on the November mid-term elections where Republicans hope to pick up the six seats they need to take the Senate. The public approval of Congress has not improved and still stands at an all-time record low. Don't look for passage of major new labor and employment laws before the November elections, although there may be "messaging" votes taken on election year issues designed to highlight the two parties' policy differences for reelection purposes. Piecemeal immigration reform and multi-employer pension reforms still remain a possibility, but time is running out before the scheduled October 2 early Congressional adjournment to campaign.

*December 2013*

*About the author and firm

Harold P. Coxson is a principal with Ogletree Governmental Affairs, Inc. and a shareholder in the Washington, D.C. office of Ogletree, Deakins, Nash, Smoak & Stewart, P.C. (Ogletree Deakins), where he Chairs the firm's Government Relations Practice Group. Ogletree Deakins is a law firm with over 700 lawyers in 45 cities in the United States and in Europe. The firm represents employers exclusively in all aspects of labor and employment law. For additional information about Ogletree Deakins visit its website at http://www.ogletreedeakins.com.

*This article was written by Ogletree Deakins, a labor and employment law firm that represents management. This information should not be relied upon as legal advice.*

# Chapter 4

## Your 14 Labor and Employment Resolutions for 2014

by Alizah Z. Diamond*

Our government managed to reach a deal to avoid another government shutdown. And so, while our tax refunds will continue to be processed and parks remain open, it is that time of year again—the time to review and reflect on all that has happened this past year and to look ahead to new possibilities in the upcoming year. What resolutions will we make for 2014? Will we learn to sit at the dinner table with our families and not look at our smart phones? Resolve not to bring cookies into the house (for, at least, most of the week)? Take mass transit, however unpredictable, instead of spending too much money on tolls and gas? Clean out the garage?

While ambiguity in the application and implementation of the federal Affordable Care Act (ACA) has dominated the labor and employment arena for many employers this year, employers should not be caught unaware of the other significant labor and employment issues that arose in 2013 and that will impact them in the New Year. To help employers gain an understanding of, and a solid foundation to navigate successfully through, a number of these issues, we encourage employers to consider making the following resolutions:

1. **For employers with 50 or more employees that offer company-sponsored health insurance plans, prepare to provide health care coverage to eligible workers within 90 days of employment, and also make sure the plan(s) meets the requirements set forth under the ACA.** For employers with more than 100 employees, the mandate will go into effect in early 2015 (but such businesses will only need to offer coverage to 70% of their full-time employees until 2016, at which point they must begin offering coverage to 95% of such employees). For

employers with between 50 and 100 employees, the mandate to provide ACA-compatible health insurance to employees has been postponed until 2016. All employers should watch for the U.S. Supreme Court's decision, expected before July 2014, regarding the legality of the ACA's requirement that all companies cover certain reproductive health services without co-pays.

2. **Prepare for minimum wage increases that will go into effect on January 1, 2014** if you are an employer in the one of the following states: Arizona, California, Colorado, Connecticut, Florida, Missouri, Montana, New Jersey, New York, Ohio, Oregon, Rhode Island, Vermont and Washington. The minimum wage in Massachusetts is also set to increase on July 1, 2014. Be aware that several states have already approved additional increases that will go into effect in 2015 and/or 2016.

3. **Develop a "Bring Your Own Device" (BYOD) policy, or enhance your existing policy, to address issues relating to employees' increasing use of their own electronic devices, such as smartphones and tablets, to connect to company networks and to store and process company information.** Among other things, a BYOD policy should identify the employees eligible to use their own devices and permitted devices, and set parameters regarding access to company information and mandatory authorization, password protection, data ownership, risky applications, third-party storage, employee privacy, confidentiality and required safety precautions.

4. **Review and update employee and applicant criminal background check policies and practices to ensure that they are directly job related and conducted on an individualized basis in consideration of the Equal Employment Opportunity Commission's (EEOC) significant push this year to enforce its 2012 enforcement guidelines.** Despite recent federal court decisions criticizing the EEOC's approach and permitting "careful and appropriate use" of criminal history and credit information, the EEOC is expected to continue imposing its pressure on employers and file more disparate impact lawsuits challenging background check practices. Employers also should be more alert to the EEOC's new aggressive investigative tactics, including the use of work and office e-mail addresses of employees to collect information

during work hours to use against employers being investigated. Also, be aware of state and local laws, including "ban the box" enactments that restrict or prohibit the use of criminal background checks.

5. **For employers that are federal contractors or subcontractors, prepare to comply, as of March 2014, with new regulations from the Office of Federal Contract Compliance Programs.** These regulations require federal contractors and subcontractors to, among other things, demonstrate that they are satisfying the government-recommended hiring goals of 7 percent for disabled workers and 8 percent for veterans, or otherwise establish that they have made good faith efforts to meet these hiring goals. Federal agency employers must also comply with U.S. Department of Labor's (DOL) final rules, effective March 2014, updating the Vietnam Era Veteran's Readjustment Assistance Act (VEVRAA) and Section 503 of the Rehabilitation Act to improve hiring and employment of veterans and people with disabilities.

6. **Review and update employee handbooks, policies, procedures and practices to ensure compliance with the many new state and local laws, regulations and judicial decisions issued this year regulating key employment issues, including:**

- criminal background and credit checks;
- immigration documentation and retaliation;
- discrimination against employees based on sexual orientation and/or transgender;
- mandatory arbitration agreements;
- accommodating pregnant employees and employees who suffer from medical conditions related to pregnancy and childbirth;
- permissible wage deductions;
- employee leaves;
- employee access to personnel records;

- providing meal periods and rest and lactation breaks;
- employer monitoring and disciplining related to social media;
- employee privacy; and
- retaliation against whistleblowers.

7. **Review and update your employee benefit plans, policies, administration and operations to ensure compliance with guidance issued by the IRS and DOL following the U.S. Supreme Court's decision in *U.S. v. Windsor*, holding that Section 3 of the Defense of Marriage Act (DOMA) was unconstitutional because its definitions of "marriage" and "spouse" violate principles of equal protection under the law.** Among other things, the agency guidance, IRS Revenue Ruling 2013-17 and DOL Technical Release No. 2013-04, provide that, for federal tax purposes and for all purposes under the Internal Revenue Code and ERISA, the terms "spouse" and "marriage" should be read to include same-sex marriages that are legally recognized under any state law. Employers should also consider the recently issued IRS Notice 2014-1, which addresses specific issues for same-sex spouses arising under cafeteria plans, flexible spending arrangements and health savings accounts.

8. **Review payroll card and direct deposit compensation procedures and practices to ensure compliance with the Consumer Financial Protection Bureau's (CFPB) October 2013 Bulletin regarding application of the Electronic Fund Transfer Act and its implementing Regulation E to distribution of wages through payroll cards.** According to the Bulletin, while employers may offer employees the option of receiving their wages on a payroll card or by some other means, they may not require employees to receive wages only on a payroll card of the employer's choosing. Other conditions on the use of payroll cards include, without limitation, disclosure of fees charged by financial institutions in connection with the card, limitation on liability and the type of transfers, periodic account statements and prompt error resolution. Federal law also permits employers, in the alternative, to require direct deposit of wages by electronic means, but only if the employee can choose the institution that will receive the deposit. Employers must also

comply with their state's laws governing permissible alternative wage payment method(s), many of which still require employers to offer employees paper checks or make printers available to make hard copies of electronic paystubs.

9. **Prepare for final regulations from the DOL's Occupational Safety and Health Administration (OSHA) modifying recordkeeping requirements to improve tracking of workplace injuries and illnesses.** Among other things, OSHA's proposed rule would require certain employers to submit data about workplace injuries and illnesses to OSHA for publication on a publicly-available electronic database.

10. **Review worker employee and Independent Contractor classifications to ensure that workers are properly classified under the varying standards applied by the IRS, the DOL and the at least 16 state agencies that have now joined the IRS and DOL worker misclassification initiative** through which federal and state agencies partner on communications, training and coordination of investigations and enforcement.

11. **Review and update social networking and media policies and practices to consider the National Labor Relations Board's (NLRB) 2012 advice memorandum and subsequent increasingly intrusive decisions severely limiting employers' ability to fire employees for complaining about employers on social media, such as blogs, Facebook and Twitter, etc.** According to the NLRB, such terminations may violate employees' rights, even in nonunion workplaces, to discuss their working conditions and other terms of employment with other employees and to engage in "concerted activity" under Section 7 of the National Labor Relations Act (NLRA). While employers technically still have the right to create and enforce policies prohibiting their employees from disparaging the employer or its customers, the rights of the employees under the NLRA must be considered.

12. **Review existing employee restrictive covenant provisions or agreements to ensure that the post-employment restrictions are legally enforceable in your state(s).** While fewer than half of the states have laws on the books expressly governing non-competition agreements, courts in other states may nonetheless choose not to enforce such agree-

ments where the employer cannot demonstrate that the agreements protect the employers' legitimate business interests and are reasonable in time or scope.

13. **Prepare for the U.S. Supreme Court's consideration of the Administrative Review Board's (ARB) attempt to expand coverage of the anti-retaliation provision of the Sarbanes-Oxley Act to whistleblowers who are employees of private contractors doing work for public companies.** This issue was recently debated before the Supreme Court in the case *Lawson v. FMR LLC* (Docket No. 12-3). Among other things, the justices grappled with the possible limits of the statute's reach, including whether expanding the protection in the manner advocated by the petitioners would go so far as to cover domestic employees, such as gardeners and housekeepers, of public company officers. A decision is expected in the first half of 2014.

14. **Schedule an internal compliance audit of your labor and employment law policies and procedures with counsel,** being careful to maximize the protection of the audit results by the attorney-client privilege. The failure to comply with the new and existing legal requirements referred to above could cost your organization monetary penalties and other sanctions on top of back pay liability to employees, where applicable, and negative publicity.

*December 2013*

*<u>About the author and firm</u>

Schnader Harrison Segal & Lewis LLP is a national law firm of approximately 170 attorneys who serve regional, national and international clients, including large corporations, start-ups, entrepreneurs and individuals. The firm represents clients in complex litigation, commercial transactions and wealth management matters in more than 40 industries and specialties.

*This summary of legal issues is published for informational purposes only. It does not dispense legal advice or create an attorney-client relationship with those who read it. Readers should obtain professional legal advice before taking any legal action. For more information about*

*Schnader's Labor and Employment Practices Group or to speak with a member of the Firm, please contact: Alizah Z. Diamond, 212-973-8110, adiamond@schnader.com; Anne E. Kane, Co-Chair, 215-751-2397, akane@schnader.com; Michael J. Wietrzychowski, Co-Chair, 856-482-5723, 215-751-2823, mwietrzychowski@schnader.com.*

# Chapter 5

## Welcome 2014: Five Employment Law Trends You Need to Know

by Kristin L. Oliveira*

Now that the new year has arrived, we cast an eye forward to examine employment issues that could impact your workplace in the new year. Based on our review of what's developing from the legislatures to the boardroom, these are five hot topics that we think are worthy of watching:

### 1. *Will "Ban the Box" measures affect your workplace?*

"Ban the Box" laws are gaining steam across the country. Generally, ban the box initiatives eliminate the question about criminal convictions from a job application or interview. Instead, an employer may only ask about an applicant's criminal history once it determines the applicant is qualified for the position. Advocates for these measures argue that by delaying the inquiry, employers are not automatically disqualifying candidates based solely upon a criminal history. Some ban the box measures require the employer to consider the nature of the conviction and the relationship of the conviction to the job before disqualifying the employee due to a criminal background. Ban the box laws, advocates argue, reduce barriers to employment for individuals with criminal histories, decrease unemployment in communities with concentrated numbers of previous offenders, and ensure fairness for those with outdated or minor convictions.

Currently over 50 jurisdictions, including states, counties and cities, have taken steps to limit an employer's consideration of criminal history and convictions in the hiring process. Six states have enacted some type of ban the box measure in 2013 alone. In California, Governor Brown signed AB 218, adding Section 432.9 to the California Labor Code, in

October 2013. Effective on July 1, 2014, Section 432.9 prohibits government agencies from asking job applicants about criminal convictions until the agency has determined that the applicant meets minimum qualifications for the job. The new law applies only to public employers. The City of Richmond in Northern California took a bigger step to ban the box by passing a local ordinance effective in September 2013 that prohibits city contractors from ever inquiring about applicants' criminal histories. The Richmond ordinance states that private companies with city contracts and more than nine employees cannot ask about an applicant's criminal record. If employers ask, they stand to lose their city contracts. The ordinance makes exceptions for jobs that the city government deems sensitive and allows criminal background checks for certain positions, such as those within the police department and schools, for which federal or state law requires them.

With the passage of AB 218, California joins nine other states in adopting ban the box laws. Hawaii, Massachusetts, Minnesota and Rhode Island are the four states that have banned private employers from inquiring about an applicant's criminal background until the applicant is deemed qualified for the position. Some criminal reform advocates view AB 218 as a harbinger of the California legislature taking action to bar private employers from asking about any criminal convictions in the hiring process.

The use of criminal background checks in employment has also come under fire by the Equal Employment Opportunity Commission as we earlier discussed, although the federal agency has not been wholly successful in arguing criminal backgrounds checks are discriminatory.

**What To Do in 2014:** Stay tuned, as more ban the box laws are expected in the coming year.

**2. *Do you use independent contractors in your workplace?***

Another hot topic worthy of attention is the governmental crackdown on the misuse of independent contractors and the increase in the number of class actions seeking millions of dollars in wages and penalties related to the misclassification of employees as independent contractors. The press is monitoring these developments, and the *New York Times* recently published an opinion piece about the effect of misclassification on the individual worker.

In November 2013, U.S. Senator Bob Casey (D-PA) introduced the Payroll Fraud Prevention Act of 2013, which was similar to a federal bill introduced, but not enacted, in 2010. The legislation is designed to make the misclassification of employees as independent contractors a specific violation of the Fair Labor Standards Act. Currently, the Fair Labor Standards Act only allows workers who should have been classified as employees to recover minimum wages that they should have been paid, including overtime, and penalties. Senator Casey's proposed bill would enable the U.S. Department of Labor (DOL) to clamp down on companies that misclassify workers as independent contractors to reduce payroll and tax obligations. The bill would also impact companies that unintentionally misclassify workers, and enable the DOL to increase audits of companies operating in industries, like construction, where misclassification commonly occurs. Lastly, employers would be liable if they discriminate against a person who has opposed any practice or filed a complaint relating to misclassification.

Even if the Payroll Fraud Prevention Act does not ultimately become federal law, it is clear that federal and state agencies are focusing their resources on investigating worker misclassification. In November 2013, the DOL entered into partnership agreements with New York state agencies to allow the federal and state agencies to coordinate investigations and joint enforcement activities, exchange investigative leads, complaints and referrals of possible violations, and share confidential unemployment compensation information, all designed to find improperly classified workers. New York became the fifteenth state to enter into such an arrangement with the DOL. California's Secretary of Labor and the DOL signed a similar agreement in December 2011. In addition, the DOL is actively pursuing wage claims on behalf of those who have been misclassified. In December 2013, the federal agency filed a lawsuit against a Georgia restaurant and the restaurant's owner seeking $2 million in wages and liquidated damages for servers who were wrongly misclassified as independent contractors and thus were not paid minimum wage and overtime. The IRS has expressed its intent to focus on misclassification issues, and the resulting loss of federal payroll taxes, beginning in the first quarter of 2014.

The plaintiff's bar has taken notice as well. High profile misclassification class action cases include a California lawsuit against AT&T, Apple and a staffing agency by customer service representatives who claimed they were misclassified as independent contractors, ending in a $1.24 million settlement in early 2013. Two months ago, a Massachusetts federal judge approved a $7.5 million class action settlement for claims that an office cleaning company misclassified employees as independent contractors. Liability for misclassification results not only from regulatory enforcement, but expensive class action lawsuits when companies improperly classify an entire category of workers.

**What To Do in 2014:** With the increased focus on classification issues, companies should be proactive in periodically evaluating workers' classifications to ensure they comply with federal and state law.

**3. *Does your workplace offer employee wellness plans?***

The Patient Protection and Affordable Care Act (ACA)—often called "Obamacare"—creates new financial incentives for employers to implement or build upon existing wellness programs. Many employers already offer wellness plans for their employees. However, the offering of wellness plans is expected to surge in 2014 as employers will be able to give larger rewards under the ACA, including the reduction of insurance premiums, to participating employees. Looking ahead, employers who offer wellness plans should be mindful of the potential legal issues arising under these plans.

There are two types of wellness plans: participatory wellness programs and health-contingent programs. The DOL has adopted rules governing the implementation of the wellness plans. Participatory wellness programs are the most popular and are available without regard to an individual's health status. Examples include reimbursement for gym membership fees, a reward for attending free health education or nutritional seminars, or a program rewarding employees who complete a health risk assessment without requiring further action. The employee need only complete the program to obtain the reward. The reward is not outcome-based. To ensure participatory plans are nondiscriminatory and comply with the ACA, they must be made available to all similarly situated employees without regard to health status.

On the other hand, health-contingent wellness programs generally require individuals to either meet a specific standard related to their health or complete an activity to obtain a reward. Examples of health-contingent wellness plans include rewards for those who successfully complete smoking cessation programs or achieve a particular cholesterol level, weight or other biometric standard. Employers should be mindful of the DOL's rules in developing nondiscriminatory health-contingent wellness programs. As we discussed here, there are uncertainties surrounding the implementation of health-contingent wellness programs that comply with the discriminatory and privacy provisions of several laws, including the ACA, Title VII of the Civil Rights Act, the Americans with Disabilities Act, and the Genetic Information Non-Discrimination Act.

**What To Do in 2014:** While we wait for more guidance from federal agencies on avoiding discrimination claims in the use of health-contingent wellness plans, employers should consider offering reasonable accommodations, absent undue hardship, to employees who cannot meet wellness plan requirements due to a disability. To avoid exposure for discrimination claims in this period of uncertainty, employers may wish to offer incentives to encourage healthy behaviors, rather than penalize employees for failing to meet certain health goals.

4. ***Are you reading Facebook or other social media websites to make hiring decisions?***

Use of social media to share photographs, personal details, thoughts, and opinions on each and every subject is prevalent. And, there is no question that employers regularly review social media postings and other online sources as part of the hiring process. A recent study from Carnegie Mellon University concluded that employers use social networks to find evidence of unprofessional behavior, including complaints about previous employers or discussion of drug use.

As of January 2013, the California Labor Code prohibits employers from requesting or requiring applicants or employees to (1) disclose social media log-in credentials; (2) access personal social media in the employer's presence; or, (3) divulge any personal social media, except in limited cases. California joins eleven other states that regulate an employer's ability to request passwords to individuals' social media accounts and prevent an employer from demanding that an applicant or employee log on to a social media profile to allow the employer to "shoulder surf" and review the information contained in those profiles.

Still, questions persist about the propriety of social media in the hiring process when candidates have not made their social media profiles "private." In those instances, an employer may lawfully check online photographs and profiles observing how candidates spend their time, what they like or dislike, and other items that may reveal a candidate's race, ethnicity, marital status, disability status, or other information that you would not dream about asking in a job interview. Simply reading this publicly-available information does not violate employment laws. It is what you do with the information you either intentionally or inadvertently discover that can cause headaches. Of course, making employment decisions based on an individual's protected characteristics, such as marital status, age, perceived or actual disability, race, veteran status, etc., will run afoul of equal employment laws. But, what if you learn of a particular characteristic, like a disability, and allow that to influence your employment decision?

On balance, checking social media websites as part of the hiring process is rife with legal risks. Even if you do not make a decision based upon an impermissible reason, it is difficult to defend a hiring decision when in the process of reading social media, you learn of a characteristic you would not typically know from an employee interview, such as an employee's religion, disability, or marital status. Using social media to research candidates may increase the risk of an applicant claiming discrimination in the hiring process and expose you to unintended legal liabilities.

**What To Do in 2014:** If you must "Google" an applicant or scan his or her Facebook public profile, consider the following steps to limit exposure:

- First, ask yourself why are you researching this individual online? Is it integral to the hiring process? Can you obtain the necessary information from interviews and reference checks, or other materials?

- Interview the applicant first before reviewing social media profiles. This will allow you to focus on the applicant's qualifications and experience.

- If you are conducting a background check prior to hiring, you should disclose to the applicant that the background check will include review of social media websites.

- It is prudent to have someone other than the final decision-maker (ideally, a third-party provider who is in the business of performing background checks) to consult the social media websites equipped with a specific list of information to legally consider. The reviewer should not make notes of information that may relate to a protected characteristic.

- If you utilize a background check policy that includes consultation of social media, be sure to apply that policy evenly and consistently with all candidates to avoid claims of differential treatment.

- It is a good idea to keep all records, including the webpages you reviewed, of your hiring decision. These records will support your defense to any possible claim that you failed to hire someone based on a discriminatory or unlawful reason.

### 5. *Does your workplace need a "Bring Your Own Device" (BYOD) Policy?*

A Cisco study published in 2013 found that 90 percent of Americans use their own smartphones for work purposes. Workers prefer to use their own personal devices that may be more cutting edge and user-friendly then equipment provided by the company. And workers are reluctant to carry multiple laptops and telephones, some designed for personal use and others for work purposes. When employees wish to perform work activities on their own personal mobile devices, like laptops, iPads, and iPhones, how do companies minimize the risk of disclosure of sensitive confidential information, data breaches, or other issues regarding access to private employer data on an employee's personal device? What happens if your employee leaves his personal iPad that contains proprietary research and development on an airplane? How does a company respond when its sensitive data is on the employee's personal device when the employee leaves, particularly if the employee is moving to a competitor? If your employees elect to use their own mobile device to access sensitive company data, then there is no easy, straightforward way to keep your company's data safe. Against this backdrop, more companies are evaluating the implementation of a "BYOD" or bring your own device policy.

**What To Do in 2014:** In considering a BYOD policy, determine the company's overall objectives. Identify which employees or jobs truly need to have access to work portals on their personal devices in order to improve productivity. Ascertain how your employees use their mobile devices for work purposes in order to understand the best way to protect company data. Work with your I.T. department or an I.T. consultant to identify the appropriate software that will allow your employees access on mobile devices, while providing security measures to protect that data. Consider using remote data-wiping technology that allows the employer to erase data or disable access if the employee loses the device or leaves the company. Inform employees of your expectations of data protection and provide a written BYOD policy to employees. A comprehensive exit interview and off-boarding process will help ensure that all company proprietary information is returned to the employer and wiped clean from the employee's personal device.

*January 2014*

*About the author and firm

Kristin L. Oliveira is an attorney with Hirschfeld Kraemer LLP and practices in the firm's San Francisco office. She concentrates her practice in wrongful termination, harassment, discrimination matters, class action wage & hour litigation, employment advice and counsel, and internal workplace investigations. Ms. Oliveira can be reached at (415) 835-9051, koliveira@HKemploymentlaw.com or via the firm's website, http://www.hkemploymentlaw.com. Please note that this article does not constitute legal advice.

# III. GLOBAL CONCERNS

# Chapter 6

# 14 Global Workplace Trends for 2014

by Ute Krudewagen*

With the year in full swing and your new year's resolution already broken, here's one goal you can keep: stay abreast of developments to get ahead of the curve, beginning with the top 14 trends impacting multinational employers in 2014.

1. Global expansion to new jurisdictions

As the global economy revives, companies will continue expanding globally. According to surveys, 76 percent of US CFOs reported overseas activity in 2013. While many companies going global still initiate expansion through standard jurisdictions such as the UK, the trend is to venture beyond. In Latin America, Brazil is still a hot spot, but Colombia, Mexico and Costa Rica are catching up. Africa and the Middle East are growing markets, while companies are expanding into South East Asia. In Africa, where financial indicators have more than tripled since 2000, Nigeria is earmarked to become the continent's biggest economy. Overall, we predict more focus on the MINTs—Mexico, Indonesia, Nigeria and Turkey—and CIVETS—Colombia, Indonesia, Vietnam, Egypt, Turkey and South Africa. These jurisdictions bring opportunities and challenges, which will be increasingly important for multinational employers to understand.

2. Greater competition for talent

The global competition for talent is increasing. Surveys rank Switzerland and Singapore at the top of the worldwide talent competitiveness indices (that is, the ability to attract and incubate talent)—the US ranks 9th. For the global employer, recruiting worldwide talent means investing in and retaining employees while complying with applicable laws and while granting financial incentives, such as equity grants.

3. Stronger need to protect the company

Companies looking to hire globally-mobile talent need to be alive to the risks and opportunities as well as the potential for complex cross-border litigation involving those workers. They also need to protect confidential information and trade secrets, drafting strong post-termination non-competes (globally and locally) and assuring proper assignment of IP. Case law and legislation in this area are constantly evolving—one example is the new Korean Invention Promotions Act.

4. Extra focus on alternative workers

Around the globe, contingent employment is on the rise, and the desire for flexible workforces will only increase in 2014. In turn, alternative work arrangements—from agency workers and independent contractors to part-timers and temps—are being scrutinized more by governments, enforcement agencies, unions and international labor organizations. The EU Agency Worker Directive, for instance, is now in full swing. On July 1, 2013, China implemented new regulations limiting use of dispatch employees, which is anticipated to profoundly impact many employers in China.

5. A more high-tech, mobile office

With the advent of the high-tech mobile world, today's workplace bears little similarity to those of even the recent past. Issues emanating from Bring Your Own Device options, cloud computing, work-from-home arrangements and process automation will become increasingly important for global employers. Labor and employment as well as data privacy laws can impose limitations that may be unfamiliar.

6. Expanding employee data privacy protection

Data privacy remains an issue of great public interest and one of growing concern to global employers regarding corporate activities, obligations to third parties and employees' data. Stringent data privacy rules initially originated in the EU, which is still revising its data privacy rules. Other jurisdictions have implemented major data privacy laws that affect how companies conduct business and treat employees. These include the Malaysian Personal Data Protection Law (effective November 15, 2013),

Singapore's Personal Data Protection Act (effective January 2, 2013), Colombia's Data Protection Law 1581 (effective June 27, 2013) and Mexico's Privacy Guidelines (effective April 17, 2013).

7. Updates to social security, benefits and pension regulations

With today's demographic comes an increasing need to update social security contributions or increase workers' retirement age. Japan, Ireland and Spain have recently amended their retirement age, and China's new administration recently announced plans to do the same. We expect this trend to continue across the globe. Companies need to remain alert of any changes, since—as in Japan—there may be obligations to amend policies and procedures to address new rules.

8. New discrimination, harassment and gender equality laws

Legislation addressing discrimination, harassment and gender equity increased in 2013. This included:

- New stringent anti-bullying rules in Australia and British Colombia
- India's new sexual harassment rules
- The rise in power-harassment/bullying claims in Japan
- The EU's proposed directive for gender equity on boards of directors
- Argentina's gender identity law

To ensure compliance, employers need to review and refresh their policies and procedures, carefully train employees and increase their efforts for workplace equity.

9. Eyes on wage and hour and misclassification

In the US, wage and hour enforcement is always a hot topic. But employees' awareness of these concerns, and of their employer's obligations to them, is growing worldwide. Case law is keeping up as well, with a very recent Korean Supreme Court case finding that certain bonuses need to be included in the regular wages used to determine overtime pay, resulting in a possible billion-dollar additional cost of doing business in Korea. France recently amended the SYNTEC collective bargaining agreement (which applies to most tech companies in France), imposing new restrictions on alternative working time arrangements and employee downtime from electronic devices.

10. Ongoing workforce evaluation and restructuring

While there appear to be fewer large-scale redundancies, companies continue to evaluate and restructure their workforces. Internationally, due to the lack of at-will employment, this can pose fresh challenges to those unfamiliar with overseas jurisdictions. However, 2013 saw a relaxation of some of the more stringent rules to extend greater flexibility to employers and revive flagging economies. Recent developments include the reduction of the consultation period for large-scale collective layoffs in the UK and changes to the collective redundancy rules in France.

11. More cross-border litigation and investigations

Overseas employees appear to be more aware of possible co-employment claims against US parent companies. US employers aiming to counter this trend and avoid non-US workers lodging claims in the US must strike a careful balance between global policies and local management. Cross-border investigations and litigation trigger yet another set of challenges, including the international limitations of the attorney-client privilege.

12. Global focus on anti-corruption and whistleblowing

Regulatory authorities in many jurisdictions are more aggressively enforcing global companies' compliance with anti-corruption and corporate misconduct laws. Some countries, such as the UK, are considering introducing financial incentives to encourage employees to expose corporate wrongdoing. Robust compliance programs are more important to reduce employment legal risk. This challenge grows when multiple jurisdictions are involved, bringing into play myriad laws, regulatory requirements and distinct cultural approaches across mature and developing markets.

13. Increasingly global M&As

Few mergers and acquisitions are solely domestic these days; the trend indicates more cross-border M&A activity. With that comes an ever-growing need for companies to understand the labor and employment requirements for global transactions, as well as relevant developments and trends, such as the UK's TUPE reform.

14. Increasingly global unions

Unions are increasingly global as well, and global campaigns are on the forefront of union activity. A global employer must understand whether it could be a target of such activity or demands from a local union, works council or employee representative, and carefully plan its global labor strategy.

*January 2014*

*About the author and firm

Ute Krudewagen is a partner in DLA Piper's Employment group, based in Silicon Valley. She focuses on providing multinational companies with solutions to the challenges presented in managing a global workforce. You may reach her at ute.krudewagen@dlapiper.com.

# Chapter 7

## Individual Employment Dismissal Obligations Outside the US

by Donald C. Dowling, Jr.*

U.S. employers accustomed to American-style employment-at-will face a significant challenge when dismissing an overseas employee who enjoys generous protections under employee-friendly foreign legal regimes. Before "pulling the trigger" on a dismissal abroad, an employer needs to understand and comply with a number of specific dismissal obligations under foreign law. Here we inventory the seven types of laws that overseas jurisdictions impose on employers dismissing individual employees. We group these types of laws into three broad categories: dismissal procedures, pre-termination notice, and severance pay/wrongful termination awards.

But even before unpacking what these various foreign dismissal obligations are, a US-based multinational that needs to dismiss an employee abroad often first asks *how much the layoff will cost*. Laws in most countries impose rules on no-cause firings that force employers to pay some sort of severance pay. How much it costs to dismiss a given employee abroad tends to link to the employee's final pay rate and length of service, and no-cause termination pay outside the US tends to run highest where pay rates are highest. Severance costs are most expensive where targeted staff is long-tenured and high-compensated; severance costs are cheapest where an employee is short-tenured and low-paid. But there are exceptions: A few high-wage jurisdictions such as Singapore and Switzerland impose relatively light statutory severance pay obligations. And occasionally a short-tenured low-paid overseas employee makes out an expensive dismissal claim under a theory like "moral harassment."

When calculating the total cost of any given employment dismissal, in addition to factoring in mandatory severance payments, always add up accrued debts the employer already owes the exiting employee. Local law dictates what these debts are, how they accrue and when an employer must pay them. Besides paycheck up to final day worked, these debts may include: earned commissions, vested/accrued benefits including vacation pay, retirement commitments, pro rata annual bonuses, pro rata "thirteenth month salary" and pro rata profit sharing pay. Some employers also owe post-termination compensation under their own equity plans and restrictive covenants.

To quantify dismissal costs and to comply with an employer's other (non-cash) obligations when firing or laying off an employee aboard, comply with all severance mandates that foreign laws impose. Individual dismissal mandates under foreign law tend to fall into three broad categories: (A) dismissal procedures; (B) pre-termination notice; and (C) severance pay and wrongful termination awards. Drilling further down, these three broad categories split into seven specific types of dismissal obligations. We address these seven types of dismissal law obligations, grouped under the three broad categories.

In our discussion here, we assume a "plain vanilla" overseas dismissal—that is, one that does not implicate good cause, economic necessity, or some special employee status like pregnancy or probation.

## A. Dismissal Procedures

We begin our inventory of the world's individual dismissal law obligations by addressing *procedural requirements* in employment dismissals. Many (but by no means all) overseas jurisdictions in effect outlaw the direct "Donald Trump" approach to a dismissal—*"You're fired!"*—and require instead that employers take affirmative steps before pulling the dismissal trigger. Employers tend to see these steps as cumbersome technicalities, but the reason laws impose these procedural steps is to give workers (or their representatives or local government) a chance to save their job. These dismissal procedure mandates split into two specific types: procedures with employees and procedures with government agencies and courts.

1. **Procedures with employees.** Many countries' employment dismissal laws require that an employer, before deciding to fire any given indi-

vidual employee, take certain pre-termination procedural steps with the targeted employee himself, or with his representative or bargaining agent. In many countries these individual dismissal steps are straightforward and simple. For example, the Czech Republic and Nicaragua simply require that dismissals be communicated in writing. And many countries grant *Weingarten*-like rights that let even non-union employees bring representatives to dismissal meetings (*NLRB v. J. Weingarten, Inc.*, 420 US 251 (1975)). But elsewhere, mandated individual dismissal procedures can be complex and time-consuming. For example, in France mandatory pre-firing procedures begin with the registered-mail transmission of a French-language letter summoning a targeted employee to a discussion meeting, followed by more notices, meetings, waiting periods, internal appeals and papers the employer must send by registered mail. Chad and other Francophone Africa countries impose looser versions of these French-style requirements. Perhaps unexpectedly, even the common-law UK requires that employers adopt in-house multi-step dismissal procedures—UK employers have some flexibility in articulating in-house procedures for "sacking" employees, but their procedures must conform to a mandated template. Other countries impose employee consultation procedures. Indonesia, for example, requires holding a negotiation session with a would-be fired employee. And where a union or works council represents employees, labor law in many places requires employers inform, consult or bargain with local representatives over a contemplated individual firing.

2. **Procedures with government agencies and courts.** Some jurisdictions impose "lifetime employment" models that in theory prevent employers from dismissing individual staff (absent good cause or economic necessity) and that require a government agency or court approve each individual firing. The government overseer, of course, tends to focus on whether the employer has good cause or economic necessity. In Japan, Korea and Germany, an employer can fire an individual employee only if the employer has good cause that a judge will later ratify in court. If a fired Japanese, Korean or German employee sues and the employer cannot establish good cause supporting the dismissal, the employee wins his job back. Law in these countries does not even impose statutory severance pay, because a wrongly

fired employee wins reinstatement plus back pay. (Germany's code recognizes severance pay only for executives called *leitender Angestellter*.)

"Lifetime employment" countries aside, the government role in ratifying employment dismissals tends to be greater as to collective rather than individual dismissals, but some jurisdictions do impose government approval steps even for individual employee terminations. In some of these jurisdictions, an affirmative government approval is necessary for an employer to pull the trigger and fire. In Indonesia, for example, the local Industrial Relations Court must approve a dismissal, and a similar doctrine applies in Iraq. In India, at workforces of 100 or more "workmen" (low wage workers), a government agency must approve most individual no-cause firings. In Nicaragua the Ministry of Labor must approve, in advance, for-cause dismissals and economic-necessity dismissals, but not no-cause dismissals. In the Netherlands since World War II, individual dismissals were illegal unless a court or government labor agency had specifically authorized them in advance, but in 2013 this was being downgraded from a government *approval* requirement to a government *notification and consultation* procedure. Governments from Colombia and Venezuela to China and the Philippines can block individual firings deemed inappropriate.

## B. Pre-termination Notice

Many countries require that an employer give a dismissed worker some notice before a firing. In these countries, firings are not supposed to be of the *"clean out your desk"* variety. Indeed, some legal systems believe in the pre-separation notice concept so completely that they impose a reciprocal notice obligation on resigning employees, amounting almost to a temporary form of indentured servitude. Most jurisdictions let an employer pay out mandatory dismissal notice in lieu, but jurisdictions like Switzerland do not—employers in these countries have no choice but to let a dismissed employee work out actual notice. Some jurisdictions do not let employers pay out pre-termination notice unless the worker had previously consented (in his employment agreement) to an in lieu cash-out.

3. **Pre-termination notice obligations.** How much pre-termination notice an employer must give depends both on the jurisdiction and on employee-specific factors like service period and contractual notice provision. Mandatory pre-dismissal notice periods can run from a few days to several *years*. Most legal systems are short-notice jurisdictions that impose only from a week to a few months of notice (unless, of course, an individual or collective contract requires more). For example, in Mexico statutory notice runs one month, in South Africa it runs up to four weeks, in the UK it runs one week per year of service capped at twelve weeks, in Brazil it runs from 30 to 90 days, and in France it runs from 14 days to six months. But a handful of long-notice jurisdictions impose pre-dismissal notice of many months or even several years—so much notice that employers almost universally pay it out in lieu. In long-notice jurisdictions, notice periods tend to be unliquidated, hard to calculate and subject to complex formulae like the Clayes formula in Belgium or subject to various tiers like short statutory notice plus long common law or "reasonable" notice plus contractual notice in Canada. In these long-notice jurisdictions, local law tends not to impose any actual severance pay—the long notice itself (again, almost always paid out in lieu) takes the place of severance pay. But there are exceptions even to this. Ontario, for example, requires both long notice and liquidated statutory severance pay.

## C. Severance Pay and Wrongful Termination Awards

The most expensive part of dismissing an individual employee overseas usually is paying out severance pay or a money judgment for wrongful termination. Putting aside notice pay in lieu (which is technically notice, not severance pay), four types of severance or separation pay obligations exist around the world, often more than one in a given country. First and simplest is liquidated severance pay, a fixed or readily ascertainable statutory severance pay amount due. Second and more complex is unliquidated severance pay, essentially an unfixed cause of action for wrongful termination (in England called "unfair dismissal"). Third, most countries tend to let a fired individual employee bring additional severance claims disputing the fairness of a firing, such as due process/discrimination/"moral harassment" claims (in England called "wrongful dismissal"). Fourth are employment contract and employer policy claims (in England also called "wrongful dismissal"). We address each of these types of severance pay.

4. **Liquidated severance pay awards.** A liquidated severance pay system imposes on an employer dismissing an employee without cause a fixed or readily calculable severance pay obligation. Employers can calculate these obligations using formulas based on final pay rate and employee tenure/length of service. Material disputes over the amount of severance pay owed are rare, because the sums are liquidated. For example:

   - **Arab countries** require employers to pay liquidated "end-of-service gratuities" based on tenure and final pay rate. In some countries these are due even if an employee quits.

   - **Brazil** funnels severance pay through a government-mandated system of bank-administered individual employee unemployment compensation accounts called "FGTS." As severance pay, an employer owes 40 percent (paid to the employee) plus 10 percent (paid to the government) of the corpus of the employee's FGTS account. Each employee's FGTS account holds 8 percent of that employee's life-to-date earnings with that employer plus past interest. So liquidated severance pay in Brazil tends to equal about 4 to 5 percent of an employee's life-to-date earnings with the employer.

   - In **Greece**, liquidated severance pay depends on whether the employer gives statutory notice: Greek employees with one to four years' tenure get two months' pay without notice or one months' pay plus notice. An employee with more than 24 years' tenure gets two years' pay with notice and one year's pay without notice. Everyone else gets something in between.

   - In **Mexico**, liquidated severance pay is three months' pay plus 20 days' pay per year of service plus the lesser of an additional 12 days' actual pay or 12 days of pay at minimum wage rate, per year of service.

- In **Spain**, for employees hired before February 2012, statutory liquidated severance pay is 45 days' pay per year of service capped at 42 months' pay. For those hired after February 2012, it is 33 days per year capped at 24 months.

5. **Unliquidated severance pay awards (wrongful termination claims).** A multinational headquarters that pulls the trigger on an overseas no-cause firing is quick to ask how much severance pay will be due, as if severance pay everywhere is liquidated and ascertainable using a defined formula. It is not. England, France, South Africa and other places impose no fixed or liquidated severance pay obligation (or they impose only *de minimus* ones). Rather, for severance pay, these jurisdictions offer a dismissed employee an unliquidated cause of action for wrongful termination (in England, "unfair dismissal"). A local court or "labor tribunal" awards a severance "indemnity" for a successful claim. In these countries, therefore, an employer seeking to fire someone without good cause will not know in advance precisely how much severance indemnity that employee might win in court. In the UK, these awards are subject to a statutory cap (which rises annually and is soon capped at one year's pay), but UK employers do not know how much any given prevailing employee might win up to the cap. In France, wrongful dismissal awards range from a minimum of three months' pay to a cap of 24 months' pay; again, where a given employee's award will fall can be hard to predict.

   An American headquarters firing someone in a liquidated severance pay jurisdiction will, of course, seek some way to quantify the employee's wrongful termination claim. Consider an analogy to a personal injury lawsuit against a tortfeasor: The precise amount of damages to be awarded is unknowable until a plaintiff proves his case and a court issues an award. Court awards in these cases tend to be fairly predictable and cluster within a range, yet no one can say in advance exactly how much any given claimant will win within that range. And unless local law imposes a cap, no one can say whether this particular case might be exceptional and fall outside the range.

6. **Due process, discrimination and "moral harassment" awards.** Beyond liquidated and unliquidated severance pay awards, many ju-

risdictions let a fired individual employee sue an ex-employer for additional dismissal damages (and often reinstatement) where the employee characterizes the firing process as illegal, unfair, discriminatory or harassing. Jurisdictions from Indonesia, Italy and Japan to New Zealand, Peru, South Africa, the UK and beyond recognize this type of claim (in England called "wrongful dismissal"). And "moral harassment" claims in the dismissal context are increasingly common in Brazil, Venezuela and elsewhere.

These causes of action are conceptually distinct from an employer's basic obligation to pay regular severance pay (liquidated or unliquidated). These causes of action seek an additional award (and sometimes a reinstatement order) on the separate ground that in firing the worker, the employer resorted to unfair or illegal tactics, or had an illegal motive. Where local law imposes specific dismissal procedures, these "firing due process" claims include allegations that the way the employer executed the firing breached the mandated procedures.

This means, then, that an employee who wins one of these claims gets enriched beyond the amount of the jurisdiction's basic (liquidated or unliquidated) severance pay award. Remedies for these claims may include a greater uncapped money judgment and reinstatement. These jurisdictions let employees win this extra separation pay because a prevailing employee proves the employer committed a separate wrong beyond the wrongful termination itself, and so deserves extra money for this extra injury. In one highly publicized May 2010 labor arbitration in Toronto, a unionized worker won CAD 500,000 for a "bad faith" firing. Sweden awards punitive damages when a court holds a dismissal procedurally unfair. In South Africa, a court that finds a dismissal "automatically unfair" raises the cap on a basic severance/dismissal award from 12 months' pay to 24 months' pay. The UK caps unliquidated severance pay ("unfair dismissal") awards, but removes this cap for due process/procedural "wrongful dismissal" claims. France assesses a penalty of an extra month's salary for certain infractions of France's complex dismissal procedures.

7. **Employment contract/policy awards.** Our final category of separation payment that an employer might owe to an employee it fires abroad is dismissal liability under an employer's own individual or collective employment contracts and policies, or non-compete agreements. This obligation, of course, grows not out of local law but out of an employer's (or its bargaining agent's) own commitments. In some countries, employment agreements commonly impose termination-pay provisions. In Canada, individual employment contracts commonly contain liquidated notice pay provisions. In Italy, industry-wide ("sectoral") collective agreements ("CCNLs") impose extra liabilities for both individual dismissals and reductions-in-force. And many US-based multinationals have issued their own international severance pay policies or else have undertaken in-house severance pay commitments in their benefit plans, equity plans, expatriate programs or previous merger and acquisition agreements. (And beyond extra severance *pay* mandates, some employers' own individual and collective employment contracts and policies impose dismissal *procedure* obligations.)

*May 2013*

*About the author



Donald C. Dowling, Jr. (ddowling@whitecase.com) is a partner at the New York City office of the international law firm White & Case LLP, where he concentrates his practice on outbound international employment law (advising U.S.-headquartered multinational clients on employment law issues abroad). This article does not constitute legal advice.

# Chapter 8
## Cross-Border Age Discrimination Compliance

by Donald C. Dowling, Jr.*

Multinationals have to comply with discrimination laws across their worldwide operations. And multinationals certainly need to comply with their own internal equal employment opportunity (EEO) policies that they impose globally. To meet their global EEO compliance obligations, probably all major American-headquartered multinationals have launched cross-jurisdictional anti-discrimination compliance initiatives of one sort or another, such as global discrimination/harassment policies and code of conduct provisions, or global training modules on discrimination, harassment and diversity.

For an American-headquartered multinational, often the toughest specific issue in crafting any international EEO compliance initiative is figuring out what to do about *age* discrimination. US multinationals' cross-jurisdictional EEO provisions tend to prohibit discrimination and harassment (and sometimes promote diversity) based on specific lists of protected traits, usually including gender, race, national origin, religion, disability—and *age*. While listing most of these traits in a multinational's cross-border EEO initiative raises few problems, the mere mention of the three-letter word "age" in a global anti-discrimination provision causes tough problems that too many American multinationals overlook.

Our discussion here focuses on the apparently benign, seemingly narrow but surprisingly intractable problem of whether, or how, an American multinational can afford to mention the word "age" in a global anti-discrimination policy, code of conduct clause or training module. Our discussion breaks into three parts: the *problem* (widespread age discrimination around the world); the *challenge* (crafting a cross-border age discrimination provision); and the *solution* (bringing international age discrimination initiatives into compliance).

## 1. The Problem: Widespread Age Discrimination Around the World

The United States imposes the world's toughest and best-developed laws against discrimination in employment, but most other countries do have laws that purport to ban employment discrimination. Other countries' discrimination laws, though, differ from American discrimination law in significant ways. One of the starkest differences between American-style discrimination laws and overseas employment discrimination laws regards *age discrimination*. The US Age Discrimination in Employment Act (29 USC § 621), passed in 1967, is the world's most robust, well-developed and frequently invoked age discrimination law, and it has few real counterparts overseas. Many other countries do not even bother to ban age discrimination in employment.

Even the growing group of jurisdictions that now do outlaw age discrimination tend to have laws that by US standards are weak, poorly conceived, lightly enforced and riddled with exceptions. Most jurisdictions that now purport to prohibit age discrimination impose no minimum protected age (age 40, under the US ADEA) nor do they let employers favor the old over the young (as the US ADEA does—*General Dynamics v. Cline*, 540 US 581 (2004)). In *theory* this means foreign age laws are even broader than America's ADEA, but in *practice* this means foreign age laws are broad to the point of being blunt: Because everyone is some age, foreign age discrimination laws protect everyone. In an age-related dispute involving applicants or employees of different ages, everybody gets to claim to be equally protected. Foreign age laws favor 20-year-olds as much as 41-year-olds as much as 72-year-olds. Therefore, foreign age laws can forbid employers from favoring old applicants and employees by offering the seniority-enhanced benefits that American employers commonly use—service-enhanced pension benefits, severance pay, and vacation benefits, as well as age-plus-service-based early retirement offers.

Not only do foreign legal systems tend either not to impose any age discrimination laws or to have blunt age laws, many jurisdictions outside the United States actually enshrine age-discriminatory concepts right in their employment laws. For example, laws in Bahrain, Oman and many other countries force employers to give all employees written employment agreements that must list employee date of birth. Italy, Germany, Turkey and many other countries let employers use the fact that an older worker has vested in social security ("state pension") to help justify a dismissal or layoff.

That said, the global trend is in the direction of better protections against age discrimination. Some common law countries including Australia, Canada and New Zealand passed tough age laws some years ago, and now an ever-increasing pool of civil law jurisdictions including Costa Rica, Israel, Mexico and all the Continental states of the European Union purport to outlaw "age" discrimination. As to Europe, EU Directive 2000/78 bans discrimination on "age" as well as on four other grounds (article 1), and each EU state was supposed to have passed an age discrimination law by December 2006 (article 18). Still, in practice most countries tolerate what to Americans look like blatantly ageist practices including, in particular, *mandatory retirement* and *age caps in recruiting*.

- **Mandatory retirement.** The United States and Canada ban mandatory retirement because firing someone for celebrating a certain birthday is indisputably a blatant act of age discrimination. But most other countries—even lots of those that purport to impose age discrimination laws—rationalize (or ratify employer rationalizations for) mandatory retirement in many contexts. For that matter, even trade unions overseas often buy in and enshrine mandatory retirement in collective bargaining agreements. Two examples are Israel and Europe:

  - **Israel.** Israel has a law that purports to ban age discrimination (Israel Retirement Law 2004 §4), and Israel's legal community talks about how tough their age discrimination law is. But by American standards Israel still allows blatantly ageist mandatory retirements. *See, e.g., Weinberger v. Bar-Ilan Univ.*, Israel Labor Appeal case 209-10 (6 Dec. 2012); *Zozal v. Prison Author*, Israel HCJ case 1268/09 (27 Aug 2012).

  - **Europe.** Mandatory retirement is legal in much (if not all) of Europe despite the "age" discrimination prohibition in EU directive 2000/78. Mandatory retirement comes under increasing scrutiny in Europe but it remains common, widely legal and enshrined in countless collective bargaining agreements. The European Commission admits that "most [EU states] have mandatory retirement ages for particular sectors or professions" (EU Commission, "Age and Employment," doc. 10.2767/16878 (2011), p. 5, report by D. O'Dempsey & A. Beale). The EU Court of Justice, the Italian Supreme Court, the UK Supreme Court and Germany's Federal Labor Court all tolerate mandatory retirement under many circumstances. *See Rosenbladt v. Oellerking*, Eur. Ct. Justice case C-45/09 (12 Oct. 2010); *Georgiev v. Tehnicheski*, Eur. Ct. Justice case C-250/09 (18 Nov. 2010); *Poste Italiane SpA*, Itl. Sup. Ct. decision #10985 (9 May 2013); *Seldon v. Clarkson Write & Jakes*, [2012] UK Sup. Ct. 16 (25 April 2012); German Fed. Labor Court ruling of 5 Mar. 2013.

- **Age caps in recruiting.** In addition to mandatory retirement, another pervasive and often perfectly legal ageist practice overseas is imposing age caps in recruiting. Employers abroad actually pay websites to post openly discriminatory job ads along the lines of "Wanted: Brand Manager age 30–35" or "Seeking trainees up to age 28." In Europe these age caps are technically illegal—*see, e.g.*, two rulings of Denmark's Board of Equal Treatment of 11 April 2012—but the European Commission itself concedes that "minimum and maximum age requirements [in jobs] are… extensively used across virtually all reporting [EU] States" ("Age and Employment," *supra*, at 6). According to one expert, in "Italy, between 60 and 70% of public recruitment ads for jobs contain an upper limit of 35–40 years. This is true also of recruitment ads for public administration, including Italian Parliament—despite the fact that it is against the law" (Louise Richardson, Vice President of AGE Platform Europe, presentation at UNOEWG (22 Aug. 2012), *available at* www.docstore.com).

***Difference in social perspectives.*** From an ADEA-compliant American point of view, mandatory retirement and age caps in recruiting look starkly ageist (*see, e.g.*, A. Tugend, "Unemployed and Older, and Facing a Jobless Future," *New York Times*, July 27, 2013).

But there is a vital cultural component here, a social gap between the rigid American position of protecting old people from the very different social concerns abroad for alleviating chronic youth unemployment. According to the *New York Times*, Europe suffers from "historically high unemployment rates—in excess of 50 percent among youths—[which] in countries like Greece, Italy and Spain [are] discouraging young people from having children" (S. Daley & N. Kulish, "Germany Fights Population Drop," Aug. 14, 2013, at 1, 6). In Europe and elsewhere abroad, alleviating chronic youth unemployment is so vital a social policy that opening up jobs by forcing retirements does not seem too harsh as long as society (social security or "state pensions") offers a viable safety net: In many countries outside the United States, the social security replacement rate of final average pay is so high that workers actually anticipate when their benefits will finally vest and they can stop working. And so even the European Court of Justice recognizes a worker's vesting in social security benefits as grounds that can justify firing old people (*see Rosenbladt* and *Georgiev cases*, *supra*). Separately, another defense for mandatory retirement commonly heard abroad is that it serves as a sort of pressure-release-valve on tough overseas rules against no-cause firings, offering employers at least one way legally to dismiss underperformers with "dignity."

By American standards, of course, this apologia for mandatory retirement and age discrimination looks weak. In particular, to justify mandatory retirement on the ground that firing old people helps alleviate chronic youth unemployment seems bizarre—this reasoning defends discrimination because discrimination discriminates. No one would justify firing people of a thrifty race or religion so as to open up jobs for those in some less-frugal race or religion, and we now completely reject the old argument against giving a woman a job that could go to a man who heads a family. That said, Americans should remember that as recently as the late 1980s our ADEA had a (now-repealed) cap that made mandatory retirement perfectly legal stateside.

## 2. The Challenge: Crafting a Cross-Border Age Discrimination Provision

In their global discrimination policies, codes of conduct and training modules, American multinationals tend to proclaim zero tolerance for "age" (and other) discrimination across their worldwide workforces. But making this claim globally can be a real problem because of the difference in social perspectives, because foreign laws ostensibly prohibiting age discrimination vary widely and allow exceptions, and because many American multinationals' own foreign affiliates persist in embracing mandatory retirement, age caps in recruiting and other ageist practices.

We already noted that every multinational needs to comply both with local discrimination laws and with its own global policies against discrimination. Outside the United States, complying with the age discrimination laws of any given jurisdiction tends to be fairly straightforward at least for on-the-ground local management and human resources professionals. For American multinationals, the *cross-border* age-discrimination compliance challenge is how to craft and enforce one single workable cross-border "age" discrimination provision like a policy, code of conduct clause or training module. Merely to mention the little word "age" in a global provision risks liability exposure even in jurisdictions without age discrimination laws, because overseas, an employer's internal rules tend to be enforceable against the employer as part of each employee's employment contract. (Outside employment-at-will, a so-called "employment-at-will disclaimer" written into a human resources policy is, obviously, unenforceable.) This means a multinational that issues global age discrimination provisions may someday have to answer, in court, to overseas applicants and employees claiming the organization denied them rights under its own provision. In one case some years ago, a group of Chinese forced retirees sued in a Chinese labor court alleging that while their forced retirements did not violate any Chinese statutory law, the employer, when it retired them, breached its own guarantee of freedom from workplace "age" discrimination.

It would seem that any American multinational voluntarily claiming, in its own global anti-discrimination provision, that it does not tolerate "age" discrimination must have processes in place to comply with its own internal rule. But too often this assumption is wrong. Many American multinationals suffer from a disconnect between idealistic headquarters-drafted anti-ageism pronouncements and entrenched ageist practices overseas. A "little secret" in global human resources administration is that the overseas operations of even US-based multinationals commonly impose mandatory retirement and cap job eligibility at specified ages. A German employment lawyer once estimated that more than 90 percent of American employers in Germany write mandatory retirement clauses right into their local German employment contracts. These days at US organizations' European offices mandatory retirement and age-capped recruiting may be on the retreat, but many US multinationals still use these practices widely across Africa, Asia, India, Latin America and the Middle East.

In addition, ageist practices abroad threaten to implicate an entirely separate danger: adverse consequences in a *US domestic age discrimination lawsuit*. What if a US domestic age discrimination plaintiff trying to prove systemic age bias (such as in a US class action) tried to convince an American judge to order discovery, or to admit evidence, about a multinational defendant's overseas mandatory retirements or age-capped recruiting, on the theory that any multinational that forcibly retires its own overseas staff and disqualifies its own overseas applicants from jobs because of their ages violates its own global "age" discrimination provision—and likely harbors ageist animus?

### 3. The Solution: Bringing International Age Discrimination Initiatives Into Compliance

Any multinational faces a problem if it has issued a global anti-discrimination provision (policy, code of conduct, training module) that mentions the word "age" while its own overseas affiliates still impose mandatory retirement, age caps in recruiting or other locally-acceptable ageist practices. Can such a multinational possibly come into compliance with its own global anti-age-discrimination rule? The good news is the answer is yes, there is a solution here, if the multinational is willing to take four steps:

- **Step 1: Assess noncompliant practices abroad.** Human resources professionals and employment lawyers at a multinational's US headquarters often have no idea that their own organization's overseas affiliates openly discriminate based on age. Find out whether your overseas affiliates impose mandatory retirement, age-capped recruiting or other ageist practices. The answer may surprise you. Some progressive multinationals have made headway stamping out age discrimination internationally, but ageist practices remain surprisingly common in many markets around the world, often unbeknownst to US headquarters.

- **Step 2: Align the global prohibition with actual practices.** Where headquarters imposes a global provision (policy, code of conduct, training) that purports to ban age discrimination, but where headquarters discovers that its own overseas affiliates may be violating that provision, headquarters needs to select one of five possible strategies for getting into compliance:

    - Stamp out mandatory retirement, age-capped recruiting and other non-compliant practices worldwide by better policing overseas affiliates.

    - Write an express exception into all global age discrimination prohibitions that excludes mandatory retirement and age caps in recruiting—recognizing, of course, that this exception all but swallows up the global anti-age-discrimination rule.

    - Remove from the global policy's list of protected traits all mention of the word "age".

    - Remove lists of protected traits from the global policy entirely (including references to "age"), replacing those lists of traits with a general statement that the organization tolerates no illegal discrimination under applicable law (*"our policy is to provide equal employment opportunities among all groups, of whatever classification, protected by applicable law"*).

    - Replace the global discrimination policy with tailored local-country policies which, where appropriate and legal, omit references to "age" discrimination.

- **Step 3: Police outsource partners.** Many multinationals have contractually bound their overseas suppliers and outsource service providers to *supplier* codes of conduct that are completely separate from their internal ethics codes of conduct. Check the anti-discrimination clause in any supplier code. If a supplier code expressly prohibits "age" discrimination—as many supplier codes do—then monitor whether outsource partners actually comply with this particular prohibition. If suppliers flout the age prohibition by imposing mandatory retirement or age-capped recruiting, then either police suppliers accordingly or edit the supplier code to eliminate the reference to "age."

- **Step 4: Ensure practices abroad comply with local age discrimination laws.** A completely separate global age discrimination problem is how to comply with emerging foreign age discrimination laws like those in Costa Rica, Israel, the European Union and Mexico. In discussing how US age discrimination laws tend to be more strictly enforced and less riddled with exceptions than age laws abroad, we mentioned that age laws abroad tend to be, in theory, much broader than the US ADEA—again, the ADEA is narrowly tailored to reach only people over age 40 and the ADEA allows discrimination against young people, while age laws overseas tend to protect everybody. This means that many ADEA-compliant practices common in the United States violate these broader (if blunter) foreign age laws. For example, overseas age discrimination laws that prohibit discrimination against the young can stop an employer from imposing minimum experience levels in recruiting; *see Rainbow v. Milton Keynes Council*, UK Employment Appeals Tribunal 2008. And overseas, lockstep and seniority-linked compensation and vacation benefits can be suspect, as can linking severance pay to years of service and offering voluntary early retirement incentives to older staff unless somehow "objectively justified"; *see MacCulloch v. ICI*, UK Employment Appeal Tribunal 2008. Be sure foreign practices comply.

*September 2013*

*About the author



Donald C. Dowling, Jr. (ddowling@whgitecase.com) is a partner at the New York City office of the international law firm White & Case LLP, where he concentrates his practice on outbound international employment law (advising U.S.-headquartered multinational clients on employment law issues abroad). This article does not constitute legal advice.

# IV. SPECIFIC TOPICS

# Chapter 9

# And by the Way, Are You a Criminal?

by Andria Ryan*

## Getting the answers, without violating the new EEOC guidelines

According to some studies, over 90% of employers conduct criminal background checks for some job applicants and over 70% of employers conduct background checks on all potential new hires. This includes many hospitality industry employers. Most decision-makers want information about criminal behavior and other related data before bringing a candidate into the organization.

The rationale for seeking this information ranges from identifying candidates who are honest when filling out their applications, to finding those who display a history of good decision making and judgment, to reducing the risk of criminal behavior in the workplace and related civil liability by excluding those applicants who may be most likely to (re)engage in criminal activity at work. Hospitality employers also do so to avoid negligent hiring lawsuits—a lawsuit from a guest or customer, for example, based on a hotel's failure to properly screen an employee who later does harm.

Despite these important business concerns, the current regulatory climate has changed. It is moving toward limited inquiry into only certain aspects of a candidate's background, and then only when the information sought is relevant to the position. For example, the Equal Employment Opportunity Commission (EEOC) and some states are taking the position that, given the disproportionate rate of minorities that are arrested and convicted of crimes, an employer's policy of disqualifying all applicants with criminal history can have a discriminatory impact on minority candidates and thereby violate Title VII's discrimination laws.

As a result, employers must rethink the wisdom of broad background check policies that are one size fits all, and instead, decide whether, on a job-position-by-job-position basis, background information is relevant, helpful, and nondiscriminatory when it is used to assess a candidate's suitability for employment. Adopting the right background check procedures is a critical risk-management practice to avoid EEOC claims, claims of individual litigants and even the prospect of class action-based lawsuits.

In light of this regulatory shift, we suggest asking three key questions to ensure that your hiring and screening practices are appropriately tailored, based on sound reasoning, and able to survive claims of discrimination from the EEOC, individual litigants, and potential class action claims.

Once you know the answer to these questions, you will be better equipped to navigate the regulatory challenges and make the best decisions for your business regarding your initial decision of what kind of background checks (or updated background checks) to order, for your employees, post-hire.[1]

**Question No. 1: Is All Available Information Equally Relevant In Selecting A Candidate?**

The scope of a background screen can be as narrow as reviewing driving history or as broad as reviewing all information contained in any public and educational record. As you peruse the menu of screening choices you should ask yourself "What are we going to do with the results?" As you answer that question, remember the EEOC's announced suspicions about overemphasizing the value of criminal history information during hiring.

**Criminal history**

Each state has its own position on the use of arrest and conviction records. Even when abiding by those parameters, there is still the need for a comprehensive, consistent set of procedures regarding the use of criminal history to avoid claims of discrimination. The key here is to identify by job description prior to hiring candidates, what kind of criminal background information (including how many years back) the company will look for and to ensure that the same level of background check is done for every applicant for that position.

For each job description, you should prepare a memo that describes the relevance of, and need for, such information and how it is related to the particular job description. Remember, it is inconsistency in the selection of what type of background check each applicant gets that can often get employers sued for discrimination. Establishing a policy and procedure to make sure each applicant for a job description gets the same background check and having a defensible job-related justification for the relevancy and need for the information for each job position is critical to defending against future discrimination claims.

### Credit history

As with criminal history, the EEOC has raised concerns about the relevance of credit history information during hiring and its potential to inject an element of discrimination into this process. While the EEOC has yet to publish comprehensive guidance on the use of credit checks, it has cautioned that:

> [i]nquiry into an applicant's current or past assets, liabilities, or credit rating, including bankruptcy or garnishment, refusal or cancellation of bonding, car ownership, rental or ownership of a house, length of residence at an address, charge accounts, furniture ownership, or bank accounts generally should be avoided because they *tend to impact more adversely on minorities and females*. [emphasis added].

In the case of a credit check, some states require an even more direct correlation than the EEOC has suggested between the duties of the position and the risk of harm or loss to the company or its customers.

Thankfully, the EEOC recognizes that credit history is properly considered where such information is essential to the particular job in question. Certain positions at financial institutions, or positions that provide access to financial assets or confidential information are examples of jobs for which a credit check may be supported by business necessity.

In addition to looking at the relevance of credit information to a particular job, you must also assess whether the credit history discovered is indicative of the kind of financial stress that may lead to theft, embezzlement, or other workplace problems. For instance, certain collection and charge-off accounts may be appropriately considered, but medical collection accounts may not, as they may indicate an emergency situation that does not pose the same risk of financial pressure and mismanagement.

As you can see, the EEOC has set a high bar for employers who wish to consider credit history during the hiring process. If you decide to begin or continue using credit history information during hiring, we recommend the following:

- ensure that the information is sought only for positions where the correlation between job duties and risk created by financial stress is clear, such as CFO, controller, etc., or where the position provides unsupervised access to your company's financial assets;
- provide an opportunity for applicants to explain their situation and the negative credit history information, and consider granting waivers based on the information provided;
- add language to your Fair Credit Reporting Act (FCRA) notice that informs applicants that they should contact your company if there are circumstances that may explain the information contained in their credit report;
- maintain consistency by setting up the specific kind of financial background check that will be used on a job-description-by-job-description basis, and make sure that the agreed-upon kind of financial background check is consistently used for every applicant for each applicable position; and
- create living memos on a job-description-by-job-description basis that identify the agreed-upon kind of background check that will be used and the legitimate business rationale justifying why the company needs the particular kind of credit information for the particular job position because of the business risks associated with the applicant's financial stress that would be found in the financial background check.

These steps will reduce the risk of regulatory challenge and will go a long way to ensure that you are using credit history information only where it is critical and relevant to your organization.

### Sex Offender Registry

The National Sex Offender Registry is a database that contains information about every person who has been convicted of a sexually-violent offense, or a crime against a victim who is a minor, or who is a sexually-violent predator. Because of this, employers may understandably have an immediate and negative reaction when they learn a candidate is listed on the registry.

Information provided on the registry varies greatly in terms of quality and consistency. It is submitted based on the rules of each state's program and, as a result, offenders remain on the registry, often indefinitely, and sometimes for very minor offenses.

The EEOC has not specifically commented on the Sex Offender Registry, but because it is a database comprised of criminal history information, we recommend that you follow the same process with this information as you do with your consideration of other criminal history. At a minimum, evaluate the type of crime committed, how long ago it occurred, and what, if anything, has happened since the conviction (both good and bad).

### Arrest history

When a job candidate is arrested for a crime and then not convicted (or only convicted of a less serious crime), both state and federal regulators have warned employers to either ignore this information altogether or to use it merely as a basis to ask an applicant for more detail about the events surrounding the arrest. This is because the fact that an arrest occurred, without more, is not evidence of criminal conduct. Carefully consider the value of arrest records as part of your hiring assessment against the risk of misuse of this information.

### Question No. 2: Do You Have Valid Reasons To Order Background Checks?

With regard to criminal background and credit checks, the EEOC's guidance does not prohibit consideration of such history, but does suggest that screening may not be appropriate for all positions within an organization. As you make your assessment of positions for which screening should be pursued, consider whether the job is one where: 1) the **nature** of duties; 2) the **environment** where the work is performed; or 3) the **exposure** to certain types of customers or clients makes it important to know and be able to evaluate a candidate's criminal history or current financial position as part of the suitability assessment. For example:

- Do particular employees have unsupervised access to guest rooms, guest property or work with guests in sensitive situations (such as a spa)?
- Are there specific state or federal standards that prohibit you from hiring individuals with a certain criminal history, such as may exist for babysitting services?
- Do employees make decisions about or have access to company (non-public) financial information, confidential guest information, inventory, cash or an equivalent, or company credit?

If the answer to any of these questions is yes, then the duties, environment, or clientele that are unique to these positions may create a need to protect the company, employees, volunteers, guests, and the public from workplace violence, injury, abuse, fraud and theft. While not exhaustive, these questions should help guide you as you review your positions and assess which ones will have an underlying business concern that would be informed by a criminal background or credit screen.

**Question No. 3: Are You Making Appropriately Tailored Assessments Of Unsuitability?**

In the background-check world, negative information that comes back to the employer puts the employer in the position of having to make a "negative adjudication" (or no-hire decision) based on the information obtained. Consistency in the negative-adjudication process is a critical litmus test of whether there is discrimination in the workplace—the greater the consistency, the less likely that discrimination is present.

While consistency remains important in the hiring decision process, the EEOC's new guidelines caution against rigidity and broad-based rules for screening candidates that are companywide as opposed to job-position specific. For example, a hiring decision matrix that screens out a front desk clerk candidate because of a DUI could be challenged for a lack of connection between the screening criteria and appropriate suitability factors for this particular job position.

Given this, you should place greater emphasis on criminal (or credit) history that makes a candidate unsuitable for a particular job position by considering factors such as:

- the nature of the job sought;
- the number, nature and gravity of offense(s), as well as surrounding facts such as age at the time of conviction;
- the passage of time since the offense and/or completion of the sentence, and any evidence of rehabilitation efforts, employment history, or compelling references; and
- other evidence of suitability, such as successful prior employment in a similar role or bonding under a federal, state, or local bonding program.

Consider developing a comprehensive matrix of consistent negative adjudication standards that are job-position-by-job-position. These matrices should assist you to:

1. Shift your paradigm

Suspend any blanket hiring policy that has rigid disqualification requirements related to criminal or credit history, and advise your managers and decision-makers that the old policy is being revised in favor of more precise disqualification standards;

2. Assess your needs

Work with your leadership to determine which departments and jobs have duties, environments and/or exposure factors that make it important to assess suitability through a background (criminal and/or credit history) screen by reviewing the essential functions of each position;

3. Define job-relatedness and suitability

- Record the duties, environment and/or exposure considerations that drive the need for Careful assessment;
- Identify crimes, re-offense rates, or credit data that demonstrate a concern related to the above, and look to (and keep records of)

outside research to see if your assessment can be confirmed;
- Decide how old information can be and still be relevant;

4. Build your screening and hiring policy

Using the job-relatedness and suitability assessment as the foundation, develop your written policy to help guide those who have involvement in hiring. If you decide to consider individualized factors, such as successful post-conviction employment history, rehabilitation efforts such as education or training, or personal references, build in best practices addressing how to ask for information about these issues, how to assess them, and how to properly differentiate unique and individualized factors; and

5. Train, train, train

A policy is great, but compliance requires understanding of the reason for the change, clarity about what is now different, and buy-in for new practices. Training is your best tool to move the organization forward and reduce risk of misunderstanding or intentional non-compliance with your new policy.

In addition to properly training your hiring managers and decision-makers about the new policy, consistent implementation of your policy is critical. When determining whether to grant a waiver to a particular applicant based on information that explains the circumstances, it's important to maintain a record of the decision. When a subsequent applicant provides similar information, you should refer to any prior waiver requests to ensure that you are treating all applicants similarly.

**Summing it all up**

The EEOC's new focus on potential discriminatory impact of neutral pre-employment policies and practices is requiring hospitality employers to think about these issues in a new way and to assess policies and practices that may be longstanding or withstood prior challenge.

Hospitality employers have found themselves the target of some of the EEOC's systemic investigations of criminal background check policies. This is all part of the EEOC's E-RACE (Eradicating Racism and Colorism from Employment) initiative, a program dedicated to strengthening the "EEOC's efforts to ensure workplaces are free of race and color discrimination." One of the EEOC's specific goals for the E-RACE initiative is to develop strategies for addressing "21st Century manifestations of discrimination," which the EEOC identifies as including arrest and conviction records, as well as other pre-employment hiring practices.

Employers in the hospitality industry will likely continue to conduct criminal background checks on applicants. These potential employees have access to your guests and customers, their personal belongings, and often credit card information. Prudent hotel employers use criminal-background information to guard against hiring employees with criminal histories that may place your guests in harm's way.

In light of the EEOC's focus on the use of criminal background checks in hiring decisions, hospitality employers must strike a balance—protecting your guests, customers, and employees and maintaining a meaningful and legally-defensible criminal background check policy.

*March 2013*

*<u>About the author and firm</u>

Andria Ryan is a partner in the Atlanta office of Fisher & Phillips LLP, which represents employers across the country in labor, employment, civil rights, employee benefits, OSHA and immigration matters. She can be reached at (404) 240-4219 or at aryan@laborlawyers.com.



<u>Endnotes</u>

1. Updated checks are appropriate when they are regularly ordered for all or a certain group of employees, such as annually, biannually, or every three years, in cases of promotions or transfers to positions of increasing responsibility or liability risk for the company, and if there

is a reasonable suspicion that an employee may have engaged in criminal conduct or had a significant negative change in his or her financial situation.

# Chapter 10

## BYOD—Bring Your Own Device Policies

by Zachary B. Busey*

Companies, big and small, spend a large amount of resources on IT infrastructure, IT logistics, and IT support. A quality workforce will swiftly crumble if individuals cannot communicate quickly and effectively. This IT burden is a significant and often costly one, to which companies dedicate a vast amount of human and financial resources. In an effort to relieve themselves from this burden and stay competitive in the marketplace, companies have started to develop and implement bring-your-own-device or BYOD polices.

### What Are We Talking About?

A BYOD policy is fairly straight forward. Rather than providing to employees electronic devices (e.g., a smart phone, tablet, and laptop), an employee simply uses (i.e., brings to work) his or her personal electronic devices. A BYOD policy eliminates the proverbial "company-provided" device. In a BYOD workplace, the company provides the hardware and storage for the information, and the employees provide the devices through which that information is accessed.

### Why Have a BYOD Policy?

It is cheaper. A BYOD policy can significantly reduce day-to-day IT costs, as well as upfront costs for emerging companies. For example, think of all that comes with just one smartphone: the phone, a charger, multiple cables and an equal number of adapters, replacement parts (who has more than one BlackBerry battery?), stands/cases/covers, and the nearly constant managing of firmware and software updates. A BYOD policy can significantly, if not entirely, reduce these hassles and costs.

It gives employees freedom to choose. A BYOD policy allows employees to choose the type of device they want. It is difficult for companies to be flexible in their technology offerings. Most hardware only becomes affordable when bought in relatively significant quantities. And no matter what the option is, no single option will ever please everyone. Just ask the next person you see with an iPhone if he or she would mind switching to BlackBerry, or Android, or Nokia, or anything besides the iPhone. With a BYOD policy, employees are free to choose their own device—relieving the company of that decision. Employees are typically happier when they are the ones calling the shots, and the freedom to choose can be a competitive advantage.

**What Concerns Are There with BYOD Policies?**

BYOD policies are a recent invention, and unfortunately, we do not yet have all the answers. Nor have we seen any publicized disputes or litigation in which a BYOD policy took center stage. But the scenarios that could trigger litigation are not difficult to imagine:

Who owns the phone number? On their personal devices, sales employees make hundreds of calls a day to current and prospective clients. An employee leaves the company, but clients continue to call the former employee's personal number thinking it is that of the company. Can the company obtain the rights to the former employee's phone number? Did the former employee relinquish the rights to his personal phone number by using it at work?

Does checking e-mail count as overtime? This is already a hot-topic in employment law. 200 police officers recently filed a lawsuit in Chicago claiming that they are owed millions of dollars in unpaid overtime for checking e-mails and taking calls on city-issued BlackBerrys, outside of normal working hours. BYOD policies grant hourly employees tremendous freedom to check e-mails outside of normal working hours, and employers must remain vigilant as such activities can violate wage and hour laws.

Should the company remote wipe a personal device? Employer fires employee for being a three-day, no-call no-show. The employer then remotely wipes the personal device that the employee had been using under the employer's BYOD policy. In doing so, the employer also inadvertently deletes and destroys the employee's personal data. Has the employer opened itself up to liability? Would a written policy, acknowledged in writing by the employee, lessen the chance for liability?

E-discovery. The ever-expanding realm of e-discovery would most certainly include personal devices used as part of a BYOD policy. This means that litigation and e-discovery holds would have to be expanded to include those personal devices, and steps would have to be taken to preserve and collect the information stored on the personal devices. The preservation and collection of information on a personal device comes with its own questions and concerns.

**What Should be in a BYOD Policy?**

Ultimately, the implementation of a BYOD policy requires an employer to balance its own security/confidentiality interests with the privacy interests of its employees. As with all workplace policies, a written BYOD policy, properly implemented and consistently enforced, is a great starting point. Areas covered within a BYOD policy should include:

- A brief explanation of what the policy is and the freedom of choice the policy affords to employees.

- A financial disclaimer and/or explanation. The policy should make clear that the employer will not purchase for the employee devices or replacement devices. Some employers, however, may choose to reimburse employees for certain items, e.g., $30/month for a data plan or a one-time, $100 reimbursement for the purchase of a smartphone with the ability to perform certain functions.

- A reference to the employer's electronic use policy, and an explanation that the electronic use policy applies equally to electronic devices used as part of the BYOD policy.

- A password requirement. All devices used as part of the BYOD policy must be password protected and settings should be set so that a password prompt appears after 1 minute of inactivity, when the device is powered on, or when the device is "woken up".

- A privacy disclaimer. The BYOD policy should make clear that employees have no right to privacy in the device(s) used as part of the BYOD policy.

- A liability disclaimer. The employer should disclaim (and the employee should agree to waive) any liability or responsibility for damage to, or the loss/corruption of data stored on, a device used as part of the BYOD policy.

- A search/access agreement. The BYOD policy needs to make clear that the employer has the right to physically and remotely access any device used as part of the BYOD policy. The details of how and for what purpose an employer would access an employee's device will be company-specific.

- A limitation on access/use. No third-parties should be allowed to use and/or access any device used as part of the BYOD policy. We don't want a young child accidently e-mailing all contacts with something like: "aad;flkjafja;lslllllllsdfjads."

- A reporting requirement. The BYOD policy should require employees to immediately report to a specifically-identified individually if a device is lost or stolen.

- A written acknowledgment/verification. All employees using the BYOD policy need to verify in writing that they received the policy, understand the policy, and agree to be bound by it. The written acknowledgement/verification should also include a description (make, model, color) of the employee's personal device that he or she will use as part of the BYOD policy.

Perhaps above all else, a BYOD policy should identify what actions employers may take under certain circumstances—for example, "If/when a device is reported lost or stolen, Employee authorizes the Company to remotely wipe the device and clear the device's contents at the Employer's discretion." Think of it this way: If an employee knows (i.e., acknowledges in writing) that his or her employer may take a certain action under certain circumstances, the employer is less likely to be held liable for that action. While this certainly is not always the case, it is a great rule of thumb for drafting a BYOD policy.

Lastly, there are a number of applications/software available that create internal "firewalls" on personal devices. These firewalls prevent the combining of company and personal data, and the applications/software provide other security benefits to companies, such as the remote locking and remote wiping of devices. Whether these types of applications/ software are appropriate will depend on a company's specific needs and technological capabilities.

*November 2013*

*About the author and firm

Zachary B. Busey is a litigator and labor and employment associate in the Memphis office of Baker, Donelson, Bearman, Caldwell & Berkowitz, PC. He represents employers in a wide range of employment law matters, with a focus on claims of harassment, discrimination, and wrongful termination, enforcement of non-compete and confidentiality agreements, and all aspects of technology's and social media's impact on the workplace. His contact information is available here: http://www.bakerdonelson.com/zachary-b-busey/. This article is not intended as legal advice, nor is it intended to create an attorney-client relationship.

# Chapter 11

## When the Playground Bully Becomes an Adult Workplace Bully

by Linda Bond Edwards and Brent D. Hartman*

The recent high-profile example of bullying in the workplace comes from the National Football League and the Miami Dolphins. Reports recently surfaced that Richie Incognito harassed and bullied his teammate, Jonathan Martin, a fellow offensive lineman. The alleged bullying included voicemails and text messages with numerous racial epithets, profanities, threats of violence, and derogatory terms referencing sexual orientation. Incognito was a member of the team's leadership council and has been suspended. Martin has temporarily left the team after teammates pulled a prank in the team cafeteria, and he has accused the franchise of having an unsafe work environment. It is not clear what role management, the coaching staff, or the rest of the team played in the harassment, but there is a report that members of the coaching staff encouraged Incognito to "toughen up" Martin. While it is highly unlikely that this behavior was unnoticed, many employees treat workplace bullying like the children's character "Not Me." It may be happening somewhere, but not here.

The heavy media coverage and attention given to the bullying in the Miami Dolphins' locker room brings to light an issue that is far too common in the workplace. Research commissioned by the Workplace Bullying Institute (WBI) and conducted by Zogby International brings to light the prevalence of bullying in today's workplaces, reporting that "35 percent of the US workforce (an estimated 53.5 million Americans) report being bullied at work; an additional 15 percent witness it. Half of all Americans have directly experienced it." Bullies share common characteristics and are typically subservient to individuals higher in the organization while bullying peers and people who report to them. Males are more likely to exhibit aggressive behavior than women, but females have also bullied co-workers, typically other women. The situation is exacerbated when high-profile bullies find success and fame. *Forbes.com* posted a "Bully Bosses of Fame" that included Steve Jobs of Apple and *Vogue* Editor in Chief, Anna Wintour, the inspiration for the best-selling novel and hit movie "The Devil Wears Prada." The success of bullies only serves to breed more bullies as younger workers emulate the style of those in authority.

A workplace becomes a "hostile work environment" when an employee experiences insulting, intimidating conduct because of the employee's gender, race, national origin, disability, religion, or other protected class status. See, e.g., *Smith v. Lockheed Martin*, 644 F.3d 1321 (11th Cir., 2011). Disruptive workplace behavior such as bullying may not rise to the level of a "hostile working environment," and may not even be legally actionable. However, employers should not overlook this behavior and the disruptions it can cause to a work environment.

While related to harassment, discrimination, and stalking, bullying differs in that it is not typically focused on race, gender, or disability. There is not a clear definition of a "workplace bully," but it has been referenced in court opinions. In *Yancick v. Hanna Steel Corporation*, 653 F.3d 532 (7th Cir., 2011), the court declined to accept bullying as harassment but specifically used the term in the opinion. The court described the "workplace bully" as "confrontational, rude and disruptive in the workplace." Bullying behaviors include all of the following:

- Being rude and disrespectful;
- Resorting to name-calling and yelling;
- Making insulting remarks or giving people the silent treatment;
- Issuing threats of a job loss or assigning unreasonable tasks;
- Constantly highlighting employees' mistakes and criticizing their work;
- Ignoring or excluding employees and spreading rumors;
- Engaging in verbal or physical aggression and arguments;
- Commenting or making jokes about a person's appearance, lifestyle or background;
- Engaging in social isolation or retaliation; and
- Tampering with personal effects or work materials.

The Miami Dolphins' case appears to involve many of the above behaviors and examples, including the name-calling, insulting remarks, aggression, and comments about a person's background. Of particular note, Martin comes from a mixed racial background and both of his parents attended Harvard, somewhat atypical of most professional football players. Reports also indicate that Martin was nicknamed "the Big Weirdo" by his teammates and was coerced to help fund a trip to Las Vegas for some of his teammates that he did not attend.

Much of the reporting in the Miami Dolphins case is now focused on what the coaching staff knew, and whether Martin reported any of the bullying to the coaches or to management. The team released a statement that Martin had not reported any concerns to the team regarding bullying until after he left the team. Part of the problem is that most bullies do not exhibit the aggressive behavior in front of their superiors. In order to identify bullying behavior in the workplace, management should pay attention to reports from other employees. Signs of bullying include an individual frequently taking credit for shared accomplishments and ignoring a person's requests to be included in meetings. High turnover rates within a department can also be a sign of bullying. Management can take extra steps to identify problems by conducting 360-degree performance reviews that include reviews from subordinates, peers, and supervisors. They can also conduct exit interviews with employees to find out how individuals were treated by co-workers.

Bullying can also be an issue of perspective and point-of-view. Several Miami players have come out in support of Incognito, saying that he did not treat Martin differently than other players and that Martin was never singled out as a target. The difficulty lies in that Martin perceived the actions as bullying, and he was negatively affected by Incognito's actions. If the bullying negatively affects an employee, intent no longer matters, and management must concern itself with the consequences of the bullying.

Workplace bullying takes a serious toll on the victims of the behavior and the business as a whole. Victims frequently suffer from mental health problems such as stress, fatigue, anxiety, depression, panic attacks, and physical health problems such as reduced immunity to infection, skin irritations, high blood pressure, headaches, and migraines. Businesses face higher turnover, lost work time, lower efforts, and lower commitment to the organization. A business can also suffer great harm to its reputation as word gets around about the workplace environment. The consequences can even grow into a lawsuit against the business. While there are no laws explicitly governing workplace bullying, it can be seen as a form of violence against employees if it includes threats. Victims who are members of a protected class could easily use the bullying in a discrimination claim.

The NFL has come under fire recently for its lack of an anti-hazing policy, especially when compared to the U.S. Marines, another organization with a reputation for "toughness," which instituted an anti-hazing policy in 1997. All employers can take steps to prevent bullying in the workplace by developing firm policies and educating employees. Perhaps even more importantly, a positive workplace environment should start at the highest level, with management showing respect and creating an encouraging, supportive atmosphere. The education process should include training provided to all employees. Employees should be aware that aggressive behavior is not acceptable. Employees should also be able to report incidents without fear of retribution.

Employers should attempt to recognize and address bullying behavior immediately, beginning with the hiring process and watching a candidate interact with all of the staff. When bullying behavior is recognized or reported in the workplace, the offender must be pulled aside and informed that the behavior is unacceptable. Employers must communicate the specifics of how and why the behavior is unacceptable and that it must cease. Employers need a disciplinary policy that they should apply consistently to all cases. Employers should also document the behaviors and warnings, along with the employee's responses to all discussions. Employers should take proactive measures while they still have the chance to manage the matter, before the behavior grows beyond their control and into a lawsuit.

*November 2013*

*About the authors and firm

Linda Bond Edwards is a partner at Rumberger, Kirk & Caldwell. She represents employers in the private and public sectors in matters involving employment and labor issues. She also mediates and arbitrates employment and other disputes. You can contact her at *ledwards@rumberger.com*.

Brent D. Hartman is an associate at Rumberger, Kirk & Caldwell. He represents clients in a number of fields, including employment and labor, commercial, and casualty defense. You can contact him at *bhartman@rumberger.com*.

Rumberger, Kirk & Caldwell provides litigation and counseling services to public and private sector clients in a wide range of civil practice areas including employment and labor law. Offices are located in Orlando, Tampa, Miami, Tallahassee and Birmingham, Alabama. For more information, please visit http://www.rumberger.com or read more about us on our blog http://rumberger-kirk-caldwell.com.

This article does not constitute legal advice. All persons are advised to consult an attorney regarding any legal issues.

# Chapter 12

## Guidelines for Protecting Company Trade Secrets

by Armand J. Zottola and Robert F. Parr*

"Trade secrets" are generally defined as confidential proprietary information that provides a business with a competitive advantage or actual or potential economic benefit. Trade secrets are protected under the Economic Espionage Act of 1994 (EEA) at the federal level, and 48 states have enacted statutes largely patterned upon the Uniform Trade Secrets Act[1] (UTSA) (collectively, "Statutes"). Under these Statutes, company information that may be protectable as a trade secret must specifically have three characteristics:

i. the information must fall within the defined "information" eligible for protection;

ii. such information must derive independent economic value from not being generally known or readily ascertainable by appropriate means by others; and

iii. the information must be the subject of reasonable efforts to maintain its secrecy.

Trade secret theft and economic espionage against U.S. companies continue to accelerate. Even a single trade secret security breach may substantially undermine a company's ability to compete in the marketplace. In recognition of this threat, Congress and certain state legislatures have recently passed some legislation that has broadened and strengthened trade secret protection. Consequently, it has become important for private sector businesses to ensure that they sufficiently safeguard all proprietary and customer information that may qualify as protectable trade secrets. To that end, this guide provides jurisdiction-neutral explanations of key trade secrets concepts, and offers pointers on how to identify and sufficiently protect potential trade secret information.

### 1. Determine Which Data Constitutes "Information"

There is no bright-line definition as to what subject matter constitutes "information" under the Statutes. The aforementioned statutes generally define "information" broadly to include:

- All forms and types of financial, business, scientific, technical, economic, and engineering information;
- Patterns, plans, compilations, program devices, formulas, designs, prototypes, methods, techniques, processes, procedures, or codes;
- Information related to single or multiple events, negative data points that have commercial value such as the results of lengthy and expensive research which prove that a certain process will not work; and
- Information that can be held or stored in any medium (whether physically, photographically, graphically, electronically, or in writing).

Courts have similarly interpreted "information" to cover virtually any knowledge, data or process used to conduct business that is protected from public disclosure. For example, the following categories of information have been found by courts of law to constitute trade secrets:

- Pricing techniques
- Marketing techniques
- The identity and requirements of customers
- Financial information
- Customer information
- Maintenance of data on customer lists and needs
- Sources of supplies
- Pricing data and figures

- Manufacturing processes
- Product compositions
- Expiration lists (often used in the insurance industry)
- Buy books
- Cost books
- Customer books or lists
- Confidential costs

As a result, businesses should realize that vast amounts of their data may constitute "information" eligible for trade secret protection.

### 2. "Economically Valuable" and "Not Readily Ascertainable" Information

Information must also retain "economic value" and not be "readily ascertainable" by others. Although determined subjectively at first by the claimant, courts of law determine whether information satisfies this standard on a case-by-case basis depending on the unique facts and circumstances of a proceeding. However, when determining value and whether information is readily ascertainable, courts of law generally consider the following factors:

- Reasonable protective measures (not all conceivable efforts) have been established to protect the information from both internal and external theft or misappropriation;
- The information is known by a limited number of employees or other parties (in a "confidential relationship" with the company) who possess a business-need-to-know;
- The information has actual or potential commercial value to a company or provides a company with a competitive advantage in the marketplace;

- The company devoted significant time, money and other resources to develop the information;
- The information would be useful to competitors and requires a significant investment of time, expense or effort to duplicate or acquire, even if some or all competitors possess the know-how and means to independently create their own versions of the information; and
- The information is not generally known to the public, or to other persons or businesses outside of the company who can obtain economic value from its disclosure.

The more of these factors that apply to particular company information, the greater the likelihood a court of law would ultimately conclude the information constitutes a trade secret.

### 3. Implement Reasonable Protective Measures to Ensure Secrecy

Information that retains economic value and is not readily ascertainable must also be subject to reasonable security measures. Businesses should implement reasonable technical, administrative, contractual and physical safeguards appropriately tailored to the day-to-day business of the particular enterprise, the confidential information sought to be protected, the community in which the company operates, and the established awareness of the individual participants to whom access to the information may be granted. Appropriate security measures should result from some consideration of the foregoing factors and an assessment of what safeguards are most compatible with the practicalities and efficiencies of the unique workplace.

#### a. **Written Information Security Policies**

Companies should implement written information security and confidentiality programs that incorporate proven information security and confidentiality principles. These programs should be regularly and consistently enforced in order to satisfy the third element of the trade secrets test. Below is a list of some suggested measures that companies may adopt to protect confidential information that is eligible for trade secret status:

- *Risk identification and assessment.* Use commercially reasonable efforts to (i) identify and assess reasonably foreseeable threats to the security of confidential information; (ii) identify and assess the likelihood of harm and potential damage flowing from such threats; and (iii) gauge the need to adjust security protocols to address new threats and program deficiencies.

- *Safeguards.* Implement certain administrative, technical and physical safeguards to prevent the unauthorized access to and use or disclosure of confidential information:

  (1) **Administrative Safeguards**

  - *Compartmentalize information.* Restrict access to confidential information on a business-need-to-know basis. These restrictions could include dividing information into pieces and precluding all but a few employees from having access to the entirety.

  - *Use unique employee identifiers.* Assign each employee with computer access a unique identification number to enable system tracking.

  - *Audit security protocols.* Regularly review the efficacy of security procedures to address new threats and program deficiencies.

  - *Legending materials.* Classify information according to type and sensitivity and mark documents with an appropriate legend (such as "confidential" or "top secret").

  - *Distribute employee manuals.* Circulate an employee handbook that (i) outlines what constitutes confidential information or a "trade secret"; (ii) explains the essential nature of the information security and confidentiality program; (iii) reproduces the material terms of any restrictive covenants; and (iv) describes company policies regarding social media use, remote access and mobile devices, and employee privacy.

- *Conduct employee training.* Regularly train employees about information secrecy, and issue periodic reminders about secrecy obligations.

- *Entrance interviews.* Conduct entrance interviews for new hires to determine whether they are subject to restrictive covenants with former employers or whether their new employment status raises a substantial likelihood that the company will improperly use a former employer's trade secrets.

- *Exit interviews.* Conduct exit interviews with departing personnel to (i) review secrecy obligations and restrictive covenants; and (ii) require the departing employee to sign a statement providing that such employee has returned all company materials containing confidential information, and understands and agrees to abide by post-employment obligations.

- *Review released content.* Review company advertising, websites, press releases, seminar content and articles before publication to ensure that trade secret information is not inadvertently disclosed.

- *Consideration of response plan.* Consider implementing a trade secret breach plan that calls for (i) injunctive relief when the perpetrator is known and the trade secret has not yet been widely disseminated; or (ii) a general exclusion order from the U.S. International Trade Commission to bar the importation of goods resulting from unfair trade practices; or, in the extreme case and as a last resort, (iii) an application for patent protection.

(2) **Technical Safeguards**

- *Encrypt data.* Encrypt confidential information that is stored and transmitted across open, public networks.

- *Technical restrictions.* Limit access to confidential information through passwords and network firewalls.
- *Run antivirus software.* Use and regularly update antivirus software on all systems commonly affected by malware.
- *Avoid default passwords.* Do not use vendor-supplied defaults for system passwords and other security parameters.
- *Catalogue data access.* Track and monitor all access to network resources and confidential information.
- *Monitor large downloads and emails.* Monitor sizeable downloads or emails with large attachments to help quickly detect potential theft of confidential information.

(3) **Physical Safeguards**

- *Guards.* Station security personnel at each facility entrance.
- *Signage.* Post warning or cautionary signs in areas near where confidential information is located.
- *Limit visitor access.* Provide limited visitor tours of company plants and facilities, if at all.
- *Surveillance.* Establish security and surveillance procedures to prevent any unpermitted entry into company facilities or removal of confidential information.
- *Physical barriers.* Lock up hardcopy materials and require key-card access to sensitive areas of company facilities.

b. **Contractual Methods**

Business relationships with parties that may involve disclosure or exposure to company information pose significant threats to the confidentiality of such information. Below is a list of suggested concepts that should be incorporated, as applicable, into business agreements with employees, licensees, service providers, contractors, subcontractors, consultants and prospective purchasers of all or part of a business (together, "Business Counterparties").

- *Confidentiality.* Establish permitted uses and disclosures of confidential information by Business Counterparties, and provide that such parties cannot use or further disclose confidential information except upon the written consent by the company or as permitted or required by the contract or law.

    - *Disclosure and assignment of inventions.* Consider coupling nondisclosure requirements with assignment of invention or work obligations. In particular, require employees to promptly and fully inform the company in writing of any inventions, discoveries, works, concepts and ideas ("Developments") created by the employee.

    - *Contractors.* Ensure that contractors are similarly required to inform the company of any Developments created during performance of their duties.

- *Terms of employment.* Require employees to execute written agreements that establish, among other things, clear policies regarding (i) the right to download confidential information onto external or mobile devices; (ii) the ownership and control of confidential information, including, without limitation, work-related social media accounts and confidential information saved on external or mobile devices; (iii) the return or destruction of information upon resignation; and (iv) the obligation to provide notice about subsequent places of employment and the employee's proposed activities or duties for the new employer.

- *Disclosure of restrictive covenants.* Require new employees to represent in writing that they are not currently bound by a covenant not to compete or a nonsolicitation clause with a prior employer.

- *Possession of another's confidential information.* Require new employees to represent in writing that they will not utilize or disclose any confidential information belonging to a prior employer during their tenure at the new company. Companies should also provide employees with the opportunity to decline assignment of rights to intellectual property created or developed under a prior employment relationship.

- *Return of confidential materials.* Require employees of the company and, in particular, new employees, to promise that upon termination, they will promptly deliver to the company all confidential materials.

- *Restrictive covenants.* Consider having employees sign nonsolicitation and/or noncompetition agreements that restrict a narrowly specified scope of activity for a reasonable period of time and within a reasonable geographic territory. The legal rules governing the enforceability of these clauses varies widely among the states. Therefore, carefully research statutes and case law on the enforceability of restrictive covenants in the relevant jurisdictions before implementation.

- *Third-party contracts.* Require contracts with Business Counterparties to contain, as applicable, and as tailored to the Business Counterparty, provisions that include the abovementioned concepts. Additionally, require Business Counterparties to ensure that any subcontractor they engage on their behalf agrees to the same restrictions and conditions that apply to the Business Counterparty with respect to confidential information.

*May 2013*

*About the authors and firm

If you have any questions about this article, please contact A.J. Zottola at ajzottola@Venable.com or 202-344-8546 or Robert F. Parr rfparr@Venable.com or 202-344-4594.

An American Lawyer Global 100 law firm, Venable (http://www.Ven

able.com) serves corporate, institutional, governmental, nonprofit and individual clients throughout the U.S. and around the world. Headquartered in Washington, DC, with offices in California, Maryland, New York, Virginia and Delaware, Venable LLP lawyers and legislative advisors serve the needs of our domestic and global clients in all areas of corporate and business law, and complex litigation.



Endnotes

1. Some jurisdictions, such as Texas, California, Arkansas and Illinois, have adopted trade secret laws that depart substantially from the UTSA. Therefore, businesses should carefully research local trade secret laws in the relevant jurisdiction(s) in addition to following this guidance to ensure that they adequately identify and protect all potential trade secret information.

# Chapter 13

## Supreme Court Finds DOMA To Be Unconstitutional—Impact on Employers Explained

by Robert A. Fisher and Lyndsey M. Kruzer*

On June 26, 2013, a majority of the Supreme Court held in *United States v. Windsor* that Section 3 of the Defense of Marriage Act (DOMA), which defined marriage for purposes of federal law as the union of a man and a woman, is unconstitutional. The majority explained that DOMA's attempt to supersede a state's recognition of same-sex marriage constituted a deprivation of due process and the principles of equal protection under the law. In finding DOMA unconstitutional, the Court recognized that the State of New York (the state at issue) had deemed same-sex marriages to be "worthy of dignity in the community equal with all other marriages" and that DOMA served no legitimate purpose other than to injure a class of people whom the state chose to protect.

Although *Windsor* involved the application of the estate tax, the Court's decision will impact over one thousand federal laws and regulations that refer to marital status. Among other areas, DOMA had deprived same-sex spouses of the rights and obligations conveyed upon opposite-sex spouses under federal laws relating to employer-sponsored benefit plans, federal income taxes, employer leave policies, and immigration. This created significant administrative burdens on employers by requiring them to treat employees with same-sex spouses differently than employees with opposite-sex spouses.

Employers operating in states that do not recognize same-sex marriage may see very few changes immediately. Notably, the decision did not address the validity of Section 2 of DOMA, which allows states not to recognize same-sex marriages performed in other states. Thus, left open is what happens when a same-sex couple, lawfully married in a state that recognizes same-sex marriage, moves to a state that does not. Also left open is what happens to a same-sex couple who lives in a state that does not recognize same-sex marriages, but who visits Massachusetts to get married and then returns home. Some federal agencies may need to, or opt to, clarify their regulations as to whether they will look to the state of residency or the state of the marriage celebration to determine if a couple is married for purposes of federal law.

For employers operating in Massachusetts and the other states that recognize same-sex marriage, the decision in *Windsor* should alleviate some of the burdens that existed under DOMA. Many employers had developed patch-work systems as to how to treat employees with same-sex spouses for purposes of taxes, benefits and employee leaves. After *Windsor*, employers operating in states like Massachusetts should be able to transition to treating all married employees in those states the same, regardless of whether they have a same-sex or opposite-sex spouse. Below are some of the most significant changes in the wake of *United States v. Windsor* that employers can expect in states that recognize same-sex marriage.

**Federal Income Tax Withholdings**

Under DOMA, employees with same-sex spouses were treated as single for purposes of federal income tax. In states that recognize same-sex marriage, this meant that employers were obligated to treat such employees as married for purposes of state income tax withholding but single under federal law. The decision in *Windsor* eliminates this problem, because in states that recognize same-sex marriage, these employees will now be treated as married for federal income tax purposes. Employers should remind employees that they may need to file a new Form W-4 to reflect their married filing status under federal law.

**Employee Benefits**

The Employee Retirement Income Security Act (ERISA) governs most private employer sponsored benefit plans. Because ERISA generally preempts state laws relating to employee benefit plans, DOMA meant that ERISA's protections for spouses, particularly under retirement plans, were only available to opposite-sex spouses. As to welfare plans such as group health plans, whether a plan had to cover same-sex spouses depended on whether the plan was self-insured or not, because ERISA does not preempt a state's right to regulate insurance. Thus, states that recognize same-sex marriage often mandated that group health insurance contracts provide coverage for same-sex spouses.

However, DOMA meant that such coverage was not entitled to the favorable tax treatment provided for coverage of opposite-sex spouses. Further, the combination of ERISA preemption and DOMA meant that employers offering self-insured plans could not be required to cover same-sex spouses. Below is an explanation of how the decision in *Windsor* will impact these issues.

## A. RETIREMENT PLANS

### 1. **QJSA and QPSA**

ERISA includes protections for the surviving spouse of a deceased participant in all defined benefit plans and some defined contribution plans. Qualified Joint and Survivor Annuities (QJSA) and Qualified Preretirement Survivor Annuities (QPSA) provide a surviving spouse access to an employee's retirement account after the employee's death. Under DOMA, some private employers chose to offer similar benefits to same-sex spouses, but they were not required to do so. With DOMA overturned, employers that offer qualifying retirement plans would be required to provide QJSAs and QPSAs to same-sex spouses in states recognizing same-sex marriage.

### 2. **QDRO**

In the event of a divorce, ERISA allows a former spouse to access a share of the employee's pension through a Qualified Domestic Relations Order (QDRO). DOMA prevented divorced same-sex spouses from having the same protection. A domestic relations order from a state court for a same-sex former spouse now may qualify as a QDRO if it meets the other statutory requirements.

### 3. **Minimum Required Distributions**

The Internal Revenue Code allows a spouse to defer the required minimum distribution of death benefit payments until April 1 of the year after the participant would have reached age 70 and 1/2. Same-sex spouses will now be eligible for this deferral.

## B. GROUP HEALTH PLANS: HEALTH INSURANCE TAX EXEMPTIONS

As described above, states that recognize same-sex marriage were permitted under ERISA to require group health insurance contracts to cover same-sex spouses. Plus, employers were free to offer coverage for same-sex spouses voluntarily. Under either circumstance, DOMA created significant tax consequences. Generally, employer-provided health benefits for an employee's spouse or dependents are excludable from an employee's taxable income. However, DOMA meant that such coverage for same-sex spouses did not qualify for the favorable tax treatment. Employers were required to add the imputed value of a same-sex spouse's coverage to the employee's income. Some companies had grossed up employees' salaries to offset this tax impact, thereby increasing payroll taxes.

With the repeal of DOMA, employers will no longer have to impute as additional income the value of health insurance provided to an employee's same-sex spouse. Likewise, employees with same-sex spouses will no longer pay taxes on their spouse's health insurance under employer provided group health plans.

## C. SELF-INSURED PLANS

The repeal of DOMA does not change longstanding law regarding ERISA preemption. Thus, except in the area of insurance regulation, ERISA continues to preempt state laws that relate to employer-provided benefit plans. This may mean that even in states that recognize same-sex marriage, an employer that offers a self-insured health plan could decline to cover same-sex spouses. However, the impact of *Windsor* on self-insured plans is unclear, and we anticipate that there will be legal challenges to self-insured plans that cover only opposite-sex spouses in states that recognize same-sex marriage.

1. **HIPAA**

The Health Insurance Portability and Accountability Act (HIPAA) governs the enrollment period for group health plans. If a person becomes a dependent through marriage after the open enrollment period, the employer must allow the dependent to enroll at the time of the marriage. DOMA excluded same-sex spouses from this protection, meaning that a group health plan was not obligated to provide a special enrollment period to an employee upon his or her same-sex marriage. With the repeal of DOMA, an employee's same-sex marriage will qualify for a special enrollment period in states that recognize such marriages. However, the repeal itself may not constitute a qualifying event.

2. **Tax Favored Health Plans**

Health Care Spending Accounts, Flexible Spending Accounts, and Health Reimbursement Arrangements are tax-advantaged accounts that allow employees to set aside pre-tax income that can later be used for certain medical expenses. Employees can use these accounts for a spouse's qualifying medical expenses. With DOMA overturned, same-sex spouses will now be eligible for the benefits under these tax-advantaged arrangements.

3. **COBRA**

The Consolidated Omnibus Budget Reconciliation Act (COBRA) requires employers to offer employees, spouses, former spouses, and dependent children the option of continuing their group health plans when the coverage would otherwise terminate due to certain qualifying events.

Under DOMA, employers were not required to provide COBRA coverage to an employee's same-sex spouse, although they could elect to do so. Employers in states that recognize same-sex marriage will now be required to offer health care coverage through COBRA to otherwise qualified same-sex spouses.

## Family Emergencies

### A. THE FAMILY AND MEDICAL LEAVE ACT

The Family and Medical Leave Act (FMLA) entitles eligible employees to take 12 weeks of unpaid, job-protected leave to care for a spouse that has a serious health condition. The FMLA also permits employees to take two different types of leaves in connection with a spouse who is in the military. Although many employers voluntarily provided leave for employees to care for a same-sex spouse, under DOMA, this leave was not covered by the FMLA and not subject to the protections of that law. An eligible employee will now be entitled to FMLA leave to care for a same-sex spouse or, under certain circumstances when a same-sex spouse is in the military, in the same manner as an employee with an opposite-sex spouse.

### B. PRERETIREMENT WITHDRAWALS FROM 401(K) PLANS

The Internal Revenue Code allows for a preretirement hardship distribution from a 401(k) for medical and certain other expenses. 401(k) plans are not required to allow for hardship distributions, but those that do must allow for withdrawal for the employee's spouse. This hardship distribution is taxable, but exempted from early withdrawal penalties. Currently, 401(k) plans may, but are not required, to allow hardship distributions for non-spouse, non-dependent beneficiaries, including same-sex spouses. After the Court's decision in *Windsor*, same-sex spouses will be able to take advantage of any hardship distribution provisions.

## Immigration

Many American employers recruit highly-skilled professionals from foreign countries. To facilitate the immigration process for these individuals, U.S. Citizenship and Immigration Services allows American employers to sponsor certain highly skilled foreign nationals for permanent residency. A prospective employee's spouse can join them in line and apply for permanent residency as the prospective employee's dependent.

Although federal immigration law typically recognizes marriages that are acknowledged in the country of celebration, DOMA prevented immigration officials from recognizing same-sex marriages performed in a foreign country. Prospective employees with same-sex spouses were required to leave their spouses in their home country or to independently secure their spouse a visa. After DOMA, same-sex foreign nationals who were married in their home country should be considered married for immigration purposes.

*July 2013*

*About the authors and firm

Robert A. Fisher is a partner and deputy chair of Foley Hoag LLP's Labor and Employment Law department. He can be reached at rfisher@foleyhoag.com. Lyndsey M. Kruzer is an associate with Foley Hoag LLP's Labor and Employment Law department and can be reached at lkruzer@foleyhoag.com.

Foley Hoag is a dynamic law firm that represents public and private clients in a wide range of disputes and transactions worldwide. From our offices in Boston, Washington, D.C. and Paris, we provide strategic legal advice that is tailored to each of our client's unique goals. foleyhoag.com

# Chapter 14

## "She Tweeted What?!"

by Tony G. Puckett*

Employers may have become familiar with some of the legal and human resources issues involving social media use by employees. However, one social media platform offers an illustration of the many evolving legal, human resources and public relations issues that employee social media posts present for their employers. This platform is Twitter, the use of which has even coined a new legal claim— "twibel"—for an action by an attorney against singer Courtney Love for an allegedly libelous Twitter post.

Twitter users may post short comments, post links to Internet sites or photos, or repost comments by other Twitter users—all limited to 140 characters. One might ask what someone can really say in such a short statement. The answer is, plenty.

A recent "tweet" (slang for a Twitter post) by a public relations executive at a large media company demonstrates exactly how much harm can result from an insensitive and misguided social media post. The executive posted the following 64-character comment before boarding a flight: "Going to Africa. Hope I don't get AIDS. Just kidding. I'm white!" By the time the executive landed, the tweet had been reposted repeatedly to the extent it went "viral." The re-posting caused the executive's post to far exceed the reach of her own Twitter account which had less than 500 followers. The tweet was reposted and commented upon negatively multiple times before the executive's 12-hour flight landed in Africa and she had a chance to see the responses.

The executive apologized for the tweet. Her employer apologized also—even though it had no knowledge that she was going to post the comment and obviously did not authorize the comment on its behalf. The irony of how an experienced public relations person caused herself and her employer such a public relations nightmare did not lessen the fall out from the tweet. The executive's employment was also terminated.

The public relations executive's experience is not unique. A college professor tweeted that "obese PhD applicants" would not finish their dissertation if they lacked the "willpower to stop eating carbs." The professor expressed sufficient regret quickly enough to save his job. In another example, an employee of an automobile manufacturer tweeted to his 7,500 followers: "I find it ironic that Detroit is known as the #motorcity and yet no one here knows how to f**king drive." This employee was not as fortunate, as he lost his job over the tweet.

In a survey by FindLaw, 29% of young adults were concerned that their social media posts would cause them to lose their jobs, and 21% stated they had removed social media posts due to potential employment consequences. In the same survey, 4% of adults reported that their social media posts resulted in negative employment consequences for them, including not being offered a job, losing a promotion, or being disciplined.

For employers, ill-conceived social media posts by employees can cause a multitude of business and legal issues, including insulting customers, libeling a competitor, disseminating confidential company, product or customer information, or workplace harassment or violence.

One way an employer can attempt to prevent employees from tweeting comments that cause these issues is through training. This is as true for the Gen X'ers who are new to the work force yet proficient with social media as it is for more experienced employees who are relatively uninformed about how social "social media" is.

Such training should include specific examples of the business and employment issues that inappropriate tweets, and other social media posts, cause. Usually, the idea of losing a job over a social media post is enough to make responsible employees consider their social media activity more carefully. However, the training should be specific in the types of social media posts that the employer or business considers inappropriate, such as: photos of individuals without clothes or scantily clad; photos of employees in inebriated states or drinking alcohol; photos of employees engaged in any sort of illegal activity (including pranks or vandalism); confidential information about the company, its products and its customers; unauthorized posts in the employer's name; negative or derogatory comments about the company's competitors; comments about co-workers that could be viewed as insensitive, bullying or harassing; and any comments that imply workplace violence. The more examples, the better this training will be for employees.

An employer also should have in place a social media policy that spells out specifically and in detail what is permitted and what is not permitted in social media posts by employees that relate to the employer or co-workers. The policy should identify the consequences of inappropriate posts. The policy also should remind employees that their social media posts may be viewable by the public in general, or reposted or printed by others even if their personal social media sites are private or restricted to specific individuals. The policy and training can highlight this aspect of social media, as well as the fact that social media posts that have been deleted may be recoverable from the social media sites servers or from the computers of those who viewed and downloaded the post.

Social media policies have come under repeated scrutiny by the National Labor Relations Board ("NLRB") for possible violation of employee rights under Section 7 of the National Labor Relations Act. Section 7 protects certain activity by employees that is concerted, and involves union activities or common interests in wages, benefits and other working conditions at their employer. A tweet about pay to employees or the conditions of working under a specific manager could be "protected concerted activity" under Section 7. The NLRB has ruled that several companies' social media policies violate Section 7 because of broad prohibitions against general categories of prohibited activities. To address the NLRB's concerns in this area, employers should make social media policies as clear and specific as reasonably possible in terms of prohibited employee actions. Employers also should include a statement that communications protected by federal labor laws are excluded from the social media policy. Another provision employers should include is a prohibition of posting on social media during work time. Employees do not have the right to engage in union activities while they are on-the-clock for the employer. This provision must exclude employee activity during breaks from work (even if paid) and other non-working hours an employee may be on the employer's premises.

Social media use by employees is one area where employers must be proactive in training and current on the evolving legal issues created by social media posts, especially given the risk of a short but far from sweet tweet.

*February 2014*

*About the author

Tony G. Puckett represents management in all aspects of labor and employment law. His practice involves counseling employers and representing employers in discrimination cases, wrongful discharge cases, wage and hour actions, Occupational Safety and Health Administration investigations, National Labor Relations Board proceedings, union negotiations and arbitration. In addition to representing private employers, Mr. Puckett also represents municipalities in union negotiations, arbitration, proceedings before the Public Employees Relations Board, and civil rights employment actions.

Mr. Puckett is a frequent speaker at seminars on employment law. He is listed in The Best Lawyers in America and Chambers USA America's Leading Lawyers for Business.

Mr. Puckett is a shareholder of the Oklahoma City law firm of McAfee & Taft. He graduated from Colorado College in 1983 with a B.A. in English, and received his J.D., with distinction, in 1988 from the University of Oklahoma School of Law.

Mr. Puckett's professional associations include the American Bar Association (member, Labor and Employment Law Section; member, Committee on State and Local Government Bargaining and Employment Law), the Oklahoma Bar Association (past chair, Labor and Employment Law Section), the Oklahoma County Bar Association, the Oklahoma Association of Municipal Attorneys, and the Society for Human Resources Management.

Here is contact information for Mr. Puckett: http://www.mcafeetaft.com/?t=3&A=5586&format=xml&p=5914.

# Chapter 15

# FMLA Leave or ADA Accommodation (Or Both)? Overview of Beyond the Basics

by Carolyn D. Walker*

After more than 20 years under the Americans with Disabilities Act ("ADA") and the Family and Medical Leave Act ("FMLA"), and 18 years since the passage of the Oregon Family Leave Act ("OFLA"), most employers are familiar with the basics of these laws. Many employee leave situations can be handled in a basic and straightforward manner. Unfortunately, others involve an obscure application of a particular law, or the thorny challenges presented by the interplay of all three laws. Unlike FMLA and OFLA, the ADA was not specifically enacted for the purpose of providing leave *per se*. In fact, Equal Employment Opportunity Commission ("EEOC") Commissioner Chai Feldblum has referred to the ADA as "an inadvertent leave law."

This article gives an overview of specific practical tips to address some of the stickier leave situations that can arise.

**Situation No. 1. Intermittent leave—taken by employee in separate intervals for particular qualifying long-term or recurrent health issue**

**How to handle?**

- *Always* require the certification of the health care provider ("CHCP") for FMLA/OFLA intermittent leave; where the need for leave is not obvious, also require medical information for ADA accommodation leave.
- The CHCP can be an employer's most effective tool for ensuring proper compliance with OFLA and FMLA. The employer needs to carefully scrutinize the CHCP and *monitor* it for:

  - Timely return (employee has 15 days to return)
  - Completeness/need for follow-up or clarification (employer must notify employee in writing of deficiency, and employee has seven days to cure after notice of deficiency)
  - The need to obtain 2nd or 3rd opinion if the employer disagrees with the HCP's determination
  - Duration/expiration and the right to obtain an updated certification (employer has right to require new certification upon expiration of the existing CHCP or upon change of circumstances)
- The employer should ensure the employee's absence pattern is consistent with CHCP or ADA medical certification.
- Consider temporary transfer of employee to a position that is more suited to the employee's intermittent leaves (requires the employee's agreement under Oregon law).

**Situation No. 2. Retroactive leave designation—occurs when past absence(s) should have been designated as protected OFLA/FMLA leave, but was not**

- Why designate retroactively?
  - Benefit to employer: reduces available leave bank and prevents "hoarding"
  - Benefit to employee: absences are protected
- How to accomplish?
  - Going forward, make sure managers are trained to recognize potential OFLA/FMLA-covered absences/tardies.
  - Retroactive designation allowed upon agreement by employee (29 CFR §825.301(d)).
  - Give employee notice of eligibility, rights, responsibilities; obtain CHCP.
  - After employee returns CHCP, go through dates of employee's absences and determine which are serious health conditions ("SHCs") (see SHCs described in 29 CFR §§825.113, 114 and 115) based on what employee reported to you as reason for absence compared to CHCP info.

**Situation No. 3. Job preservation obligations—employee is off work for extended time and employer wants to fill position**

**How to handle?**

- Under OFLA—employee's job protected through duration of OFLA leave; upon return, employee must be restored to same position if it exists or to available equivalent position if it does not.
- Under FMLA—employee's job protected through duration of leave; employee must be restored to same or equivalent position (with exception for "key employee" only if leave not also covered by OFLA; not likely to apply in vast majority of situations in Oregon).
- Under ADA—must hold employee's job, unless doing so presents "undue hardship"; even with undue hardship, must still consider employee for equivalent position, then lesser position.
  - In Ninth Circuit, even "indefinite leave" may still be reasonable accommodation, despite EEOC's position to contrary and new employer-friendly Ninth Circuit case law.
- Therefore, if OFLA/FMLA leave is exhausted and employee is still not ready to return to work, before replacing employee the employer should conduct a basic ADA analysis to determine whether ADA applies, and whether extended leave is a reasonable accommodation or whether it presents employer with undue hardship.

**Situation No. 4. Employee's medical condition is "debatable"—occurs when employer questions whether a condition is either a SHC or a disability under ADA**

**How to handle?**

- For FMLA/OFLA, must do SHC analysis (see SHC described in 29 CFR §§825.113, 114 and 115); if no SHC is present, then no FMLA/OFLA leave is required.
- If employee's health care provider appears to "rubber stamp" employee's purported condition, require second opinion (at employer's expense).

**Situation No. 5. Employee has worked only short time—employee is not eligible for OFLA/FMLA because too new, but has reported medical condition and requests leave**

**How to handle?**

- Simple (and *critical*)—do basic ADA analysis to determine whether employee is entitled to leave as an accommodation under the ADA.

**Situation No. 6. Untimely notice by employee—employee does not notify of need for leave within statutory time periods**

**How to handle?**

- If OFLA only applies, and employee did not give 30 days' or as much advance notice as possible of foreseeable leave, or notice within 3 days of returning to work of unforeseeable leave, employer can reduce employee's leave by the number of days (up to 3 weeks) employee failed to provide timely notice (OAR 839-009-0250(4)(a)).
- If FMLA only applies, employer may delay or deny leave due to improper notice (29 CFR §825.304).
- If both OFLA and FMLA apply, employer may discipline employee under *uniformly applied* policies, but cannot delay or deny the leave.
- There is no statutory time period involved for requesting leave as an ADA accommodation, although an employer may deny leave to employee who has not provided requested adequate medical supporting documentation when the need for leave is not obvious.

Although the six situations outlined above require a "beyond the basics" individual approach and analysis, in each of them the employer should: 1) always maintain open and timely communication with the employee; and 2) follow a process that considers both the requirements of the family and medical leave laws *and* the ADA, when applicable.

*August 2013*

*<u>About the author and firm</u>

Carolyn D. Walker is a partner with Stoel Rives LLP whose practice focuses on litigating and counseling clients on a wide variety of employment matters, as well as tort claims arising in the employment context. The article appeared in the Stoel Rives World of Employment law blog (http://www.stoelrivesworldofemployment.com). You can reach Carolyn at cdwalker@stoel.com.

# Chapter 16

## Does Leaning In Make Legal Sense for Employers? Definitely

by John P. Furfaro, Risa M. Salins and Anne E. Villanueva*

With employment discrimination charges at a 15-year high, employers are seeing a particular increase in claims brought by workers who are pregnant or caring for young children or aging parents. A 2010 report by the Center for WorkLife Law at the University of California Hastings College of the Law shows that plaintiffs in these family-responsibility cases are more likely to prevail than plaintiffs in other types of employment discrimination cases, with average awards exceeding $500,000.[1] In one notable class action, a jury awarded $3.36 million in compensatory damages and an additional $250 million in punitive damages when it found discrimination against women in the employer's pay, promotion, pregnancy and family leave policies. These trends raise the question of whether employers can better address sensitive issues relating to gender, pregnancy and caregiving responsibilities.

### The Debate

Some companies aim to desensitize their workforces to differences between men and women and thus train managers not to ask employees questions related to gender, pregnancy or caregiver responsibilities. But management experts—and legal counsel—are rethinking these practices, particularly in the wake of Facebook Chief Operating Officer Sheryl Sandberg's book *Lean In: Women, Work, and the Will to Lead*, published in March 2013, in which Sandberg said she instead teaches managers "to encourage women to talk about their plans to have children and help them continue to reach for opportunities." Yet, critics argue companies put themselves at litigation risk because managers will not know how to engage in these discussions without running afoul of anti-discrimination laws. Such concerns have been exacerbated by recent well-publicized demand letters received by technology companies from female employees allegedly denied promotions or terminated after "leaning in" at the workplace.[2]

**Legal Reasons to Engage**

Employers should consider the greater litigation risk of not engaging with employees on these issues. Title VII of the Civil Rights Act of 1964, as amended by the Pregnancy Discrimination Act, makes it unlawful for an employer to discriminate on the basis of pregnancy or pregnancy-related conditions. While Title VII does not prohibit discrimination against caregivers *per se*, under a theory referred to as "sex-plus" (*i.e.*, sex plus another characteristic, such as caregiving), discrimination against working mothers has been held to violate Title VII even if the employer does not discriminate against childless women.[3] Title VII also has been used to protect male employees' rights to engage in family caregiving.[4] Moreover, the Americans with Disabilities Act "association" provision protects employees from discrimination based on their relationship or association with an individual with a disability. Plaintiffs also are relying on a growing number of state and local statutes prohibiting discrimination based on pregnancy and family status or responsibilities.

**Disparate Treatment.** A plaintiff proves a disparate treatment violation under these anti-discrimination laws when the individual shows that he or she has been intentionally treated less favorably than others similarly situated on the basis of an impermissible characteristic. A survey of case law demonstrates that employers are more likely to succeed in disparate treatment cases when fulsome employee communication occurs. For example, in *Chadwick v. WellPoint, Inc.*, 561 F.3d 38, 42-48 (1st Cir. 2009), the Court of Appeals reversed the lower court's entry of summary judgment for the employer on plaintiff's Title VII "sex-plus" discrimination claim where the plaintiff, who was objectively the most qualified for promotion, was informed she had not been selected because, as a mother of four young children, she had "too much on her plate"; the court stated that "an employer is not free to assume that a woman, because she is a woman, will necessarily be a poor worker because of family responsibilities." Likewise, in *Lust v. Sealy, Inc.*, 383 F.3d 580 (7th Cir. 2004), the court upheld a jury's finding that a female sales representative was passed over for promotion in violation of Title VII, where the supervisor admitted he didn't consider recommending her for the position because she had children and he didn't think she would want to relocate her family, even though she had not told him that.[5] In addition, in *Scheidecker v. Arvig Enterprises, Inc.*, 122 F. Supp. 2d 1031, 1045-46 (D. Minn. 2000), the court denied summary judgment on discrimination claims brought by female employees who were terminated during their pregnancies or while on maternity leave. The court was swayed by evidence that management had not discussed details of the plaintiffs' maternity leaves with them despite their requests. In contrast, in *O'Neill-Marino v. Omni Hotels Management Corp.*, No. 99 Civ. 3793, 2001 WL 210360, at *5 (S.D.N.Y. Mar. 2, 2001), the court granted summary judgment dismissing a former employee's claims that her employer imposed unreasonable work hours to force a resignation because she was a married woman with children. The hotel demonstrated the work hours were a requirement of the employee's position and management communicated with her about attendance, provided advance notice of her schedules and offered an opportunity to take another position in the hotel.[6]

**Workplace Policies.** Employers also would be well-served to openly communicate with employees about workplace policies in an effort to avoid findings of disparate impact discrimination. Disparate impact may result when rules applied to all employees have an unjustified adverse impact on members of a protected class. For example, in *Lochren v. County of Suffolk*, No. CV 01-3925, 2008 WL 2039458 (E.D.N.Y. May 9, 2008), the plaintiffs prevailed on their disparate impact challenge to the Suffolk County police department's restriction of light duty work to those with on-the-job injuries. The plaintiffs showed that prior to the restriction, pregnant women had been more likely to use light duty than other officers, and women had been affected more than men by the restrictions. Employers may not be cognizant that facially neutral policies are having a disparate impact on certain groups unless they encourage employees to come forward and discuss workplace policies and issues affecting them.

**Interaction Is Required**

The flip side of discrimination is active engagement, and a number of employment laws explicitly require employers to engage with employees on family and medical issues. For example, under the federal Family and Medical Leave Act, when an employer acquires knowledge that leave requested by an employee may be for an FMLA purpose, the employer must inform the employee of his or her rights and responsibilities under the FMLA. And the ADA requires employers to initiate an interactive process with an individual with a disability who may be in need of a workplace accommodation.[7] Thus, in *LaCourt v. Shenanigans Knits, Ltd.*, Index No. 102391/11, 2012 N.Y. Slip Op. 52379(U) (Sup. Ct. New York County Nov. 14, 2012), the court denied summary judgment on the plaintiff's ADA claims where the employer terminated an employee who had been diagnosed with breast cancer, because she planned an absence from work for more than three months following double mastectomy surgery. The court reasoned the employer did not engage in an interactive process and ultimately failed to establish that granting the employee a leave of absence would have resulted in an undue hardship.[8] Notably, the ADA Amendments Act of 2008 expands the definition of "disability" under the ADA to include temporary impairments.[9] Therefore, though pregnancy itself is not a disability covered by the ADA, certain impairments resulting from pregnancy, such as hypertension, gestational diabetes, severe nausea and sciatica, are now considered disabilities for which employers must engage in an interactive process and provide reasonable accommodation.

*******

Engaging with employees on sensitive personal issues is serious business but, if undertaken correctly, can be a win-win for employees and employers. Such engagement requires that male and female employees, with proper training and support, feel comfortable broaching pregnancy, parenting, personal or family medical issues and an employee's related workplace needs. Likewise, supervisors must be trained with respect to preventing discrimination, harassment and retaliation based on gender, pregnancy or caregiving responsibilities, and they must encourage employees to raise these issues. This approach necessitates a focus on when and how to address the particular workplace needs of employees who are pregnant or disabled or who have caregiving responsibilities, whether or not the topic is raised by an employee. Employers who take the time to address these aspects of their employees' lives are more likely to retain the broadest array of a talented workforce.

*January 2014*

*About the authors and firm

Partner John P. Furfaro (212.735.2624/john.furfaro@skadden.com), counsel Risa M. Salins (212.735.3646/risa.salins@skadden.com) and associate Anne E. Villanueva (212.735.3725/ anne.villanueva@ skadden.com) are attorneys at Skadden, Arps, Slate, Meagher & Flom LLP & Affiliates, one of the world's leading law firms (http://www.ska dden.com). This article appeared in Skadden's *2014 Insights* on January 16, 2014. It is for educational and informational purposes only and is not intended and should not be construed as legal advice. The article is considered advertising under applicable state laws.

Endnotes

1. Cynthia T. Calvert, *Family Responsibilities Discrimination: Litigation Update 2010*, The Center for WorkLife Law (2010).

2. *See* Coe, Erin, "As 'Lean In' Claims Arise, Employers Must Watch Their Words," *Employment Law 360*, July 11, 2013.

3. *Phillips v. Martin Marietta Corp.*, 400 U.S. 542, 544 (1971) (Title VII prohibits an employer from hiring men with preschool-age children while refusing to hire women with preschool-age children).

4. *See, e.g., Schafer v. Board of Pub. Educ.*, 903 F.2d 243, 247 (3d Cir. 1990) (policy granting leave of absence for a child's birth to female employees but not to male employees may serve as the basis for a Title VII claim).

5. *See also Trezza v. The Hartford, Inc.*, No. 98 Civ. 2205, 1998 WL 912101, at *7-8 (S.D.N.Y. Dec. 30, 1998) (denying employer's motion to dismiss discrimination claims where complaint alleged that

employer assumed, without discussing, that plaintiff would not be interested in promotion to a managing attorney position because she had a family and the position required travel).

6. *See also Spann v. Abraham*, 36 S.W.3d 452 (Tenn. Ct. App. 1999) (no prima facie discrimination where, following the employee's absences due to pregnancy, the employer suggested the employee accept a temporary reassignment with no loss of pay and reinstatement to her position after she returned from maternity leave).

7. 29 C.F.R. § 825.300(b)(1) (FMLA); 29 C.F.R. §1630.2(o)(3) (ADA).

8. *See also Erickson v. Board of Governors of State Colleges and Universities for Northeastern Illinois University*, No. 95 C 2541, 1997 WL 548030 (N.D. Ill. Sept. 2, 1997) (summary judgment on the plaintiff's ADA claims denied where the plaintiff underwent infertility treatments causing her emotional distress, and the employer failed to engage in an interactive discussion).

9. 29 C.F.R. § 1630.2(j)(1)(ix) ("effects of an impairment lasting or expected to last fewer than six months can be substantially limiting within the meaning of this section").

# Chapter 17

# Plan to Minimize Spread of Flu and Legal Risks in the Workplace during Flu Season

by Joseph J. Lynett, Esq.*

Each flu season, according to Flu.gov, nearly 111 million workdays are lost due to the flu. That equals approximately $7 billion per year in sick days and lost productivity. According to the Centers for Disease Control and Prevention (CDC), flu season runs from the fall to the winter, with the peak occurring typically in January and February. The CDC also reports that manufacturers have begun shipping flu vaccines for the 2013–2014 U.S. season. Between 135 million and 139 million doses of vaccine are being produced and the CDC recommends a yearly flu vaccine for everyone six months of age or older by October. Now is a good time for employers to review and develop their policies and plans for minimizing the spread of influenza in the workplace without running afoul of a complex array of federal, state and local laws. This article addresses many of the recurring legal issues and questions that arise during the flu season.

## Employee Rights to Paid and Unpaid Leave

"Presenteeism" (i.e., being at work when one should be at home due to illness) is as much, if not more, of a concern during flu season as absenteeism. One sick employee at work can cause other employees to become ill. Thus, employers may find it useful to clarify policies that permit employees to take paid or unpaid leave due to the flu. Evaluating any attendance situation requires an employer to determine which statutes and employer policies apply. In general, the Family and Medical Leave Act provides covered employees up to 12 workweeks of unpaid leave during any 12-month period if the individual has a "serious health condition that makes the employee unable to perform the functions of the position of such employee." In some situations, influenza-like illnesses may qualify as a "serious health condition" under the FMLA, but the majority of flu-related absences will fall under state and local leave laws or employers' absence policies. (For additional information regarding the applicability of the FMLA for influenza-like illnesses, please refer to the Department of Labor's Q&A concerning pandemic flu and the FMLA.)

In addition to the FMLA and comparable state laws, some states and municipalities require covered employers to provide paid sick leave to employees. For example, Connecticut's paid leave law requires employers with at least 50 employees within the state (excluding most manufacturing establishments and the nationally chartered tax-exempt organizations described in the law) to provide non-exempt "service workers" with paid sick leave of up to 40 hours per calendar year. Other states are considering similar legislative measures. In addition, New York City, Philadelphia, Portland, OR, San Francisco, Seattle and Washington, D.C. have enacted some form of paid leave for eligible employees.

Regardless of the law in your state, to minimize lost productivity during flu season, employers should consider implementing absence policies that encourage sick employees to stay home, including paid time off (PTO) for short-term illnesses. Employers should make sure employees understand what human resources policies, workplace and leave flexibilities, and pay and benefits will be available to them. PTO and other workplace policies should be consistently enforced for all employees.

**Are Employer Flu Vaccine Requirements Lawful?**

Although certain states, such as New York and Rhode Island, require some form of mandatory flu vaccination for health care workers, many do not. Thus, many employers, particularly those in the health care sector, also have instituted, or are considering, mandatory influenza vaccination programs for employees. Before implementing such programs, however, employers should consider possible disability and religious accommodation issues under the Americans with Disabilities Act and Title VII of the Civil Rights Act, as well as analogous state and local laws. An employee may be entitled to an exemption from a mandatory vaccination requirement based on an ADA disability that prevents the employee from taking the vaccine. Title VII exempts an employee whose sincerely-held religious belief, practice or observance prevents him or her from taking the vaccine. In a recent case, for example, an employee who was a vegan brought a religious discrimination case against her employer after being terminated following her refusal to get an employer-mandated flu shot because the vaccine was grown in chicken eggs. In addition, the Occupational Safety and Health Administration and National Labor Relations Board requirements may play a role for certain employers.

**Employers' Rights and Responsibilities under ADA**

The Equal Employment Opportunity Commission's technical guidance, "Pandemic Preparedness in the Workplace and the Americans with Disabilities Act," includes the following directions:

- Employers may ask employees whether they have symptoms of a cold or the seasonal flu because it is not a disability-related inquiry.

- Employers may use an ADA-compliant pre-pandemic employee sample survey for employers, which the agency has prepared. It combines medical and non-medical inquiries about the ability of an employee to come to work during a pandemic. The objectives are to provide employers with information they need to plan for a pandemic and to shield employers from receiving information about chronic diseases or illnesses that employees might have.

- Employers may send employees home if they display influenza-like symptoms.

- If employees report feeling ill at work or call in sick, employers may ask them if they are experiencing influenza-like symptoms, such as a fever, chills, and cough or a sore throat. Employers must maintain all information about an employee's illness as a confidential medical record in compliance with the ADA.

- Employers may require employees to follow infection-control practices in the workplace. For examples, see OSHA's webpage, Workplace Safety and the Flu.

As the flu season continues, all employers may need to address these and other issues involving employees who are absent from, or should not be at, work due to the flu.

*October 2013*

*<u>About the author and firm</u>

Joseph J. Lynett, Esq. is a Shareholder in the national labor and employment law firm of Jackson Lewis, P.C.



This article is provided for informational purposes only. It is not intended as legal advice nor does it create an attorney/client relationship between Jackson Lewis and any readers or recipients. Readers should consult counsel of their own choosing to discuss how these matters relate to their individual circumstances. Reproduction in whole or in part is prohibited without the express written consent of Jackson Lewis.

This article may be considered attorney advertising in some states. Furthermore, prior results do not guarantee a similar outcome.

Jackson Lewis P.C. represents management exclusively in workplace law and related litigation. Our attorneys are available to assist employers in their compliance efforts and to represent employers in matters before state and federal courts and administrative agencies. If you have questions about flu-related absences, please contact Jackson Lewis Partner Joe Lynett, at (914) 514-6146 or lynettj@jacksonlewis.com.

# Chapter 18

# HIPAA and the Omnibus Rule: How to Assess Whether and What Your Company Must Do to Comply

by Helen A. Christakos*

A key amendment to the Health Insurance Portability and Accountability Act ("**HIPAA**") called the "Omnibus Rule" took effect on March 26, 2013. The Omnibus Rule impacts both companies that directly collect protected health information ("**PHI**") about individuals ("**Covered Entities**") and subcontractors and downstream subcontractors that provide services relating to PHI collected by Covered Entities (unless they fall into one of the narrow exceptions described in more detail below) ("**Business Associates**"). Covered Entities and Business Associates were required to comply with HIPAA (as it is modified by the Omnibus Rule) by September 23, 2013 unless they are subject to the grandfather clause (i.e., entered into a contract prior to January 25, 2013 that was not modified or renewed before October 23, 2013), in which case they do not have to comply until September 22, 2014.

This article will help you assess whether your company needs to comply with HIPAA (including the new Omnibus Rule) and, if so, what steps your company should take to become compliant.

## A. How does the Omnibus Rule change HIPAA?

The Omnibus Rule changes HIPAA's privacy and security rules in several key ways:

### 1. Increased Number of Companies that Must Comply with HIPAA and the Omnibus Rule Because of Broader Definition of "Business Associate"

The Omnibus Rule expanded the definition of Business Associate to include all downstream subcontractors that create, receive, maintain or transmit PHI on behalf of subcontractors that contract directly with Covered Entities. In other words, HIPAA now applies to subcontractors irrespective of how far downstream the subcontractor is from the Covered Entity. Companies that maintain or store PHI (such as data storage companies) are now considered Business Associates regardless of whether the company actually accesses the PHI. There are a few narrow exceptions to the definition of Business Associate, including: (a) entities that act as "mere conduits for the transportation of PHI" but do not access the PHI other than on a random or infrequent basis, such as Internet service providers (ISPs) and telecommunications companies; (b) a health care provider that receives PHI from a Covered Entity for treatment purposes; (c) a Covered Entity participating in an Organized Health Care Arrangement; (d) a government agency if the government agency is determining government health plan eligibility in a plan administered by another government agency; and (e) a plan sponsor with respect to disclosures by a group health plan if group health plan requirements are met.

2. **Application of HIPAA Security Rule and Certain Requirements of the Privacy Rule to Business Associates**

Prior to the passage of the Omnibus Rule, only Covered Entities had to comply with HIPAA. The security rule and certain portions of the privacy rule now directly apply to all Business Associates, including without limitation, downstream subcontractors. Under the privacy rule, Business Associates must, among other things: (a) only disclose PHI as permitted by their business associate agreements or as required by law; (b) request, use and disclose the minimum amount of PHI necessary; (c) take reasonable steps to cure a subcontractor's breach of PHI and terminate the contract if this is not effective; and (d) use and disclose PHI subject to the same restrictions placed upon Covered Entities by HIPAA and the Omnibus Rule.

3. **Business Associates Providing Services to Covered Entities Must Enter Into Business Associate Agreements with Downstream Subcontractors**

Prior to the enactment of the Omnibus Rule, only Covered Entities were required to have their direct subcontractors enter into written Business Associate Agreements that contractually required such subcontractors to safeguard PHI. Under the Omnibus Rule, this requirement now applies to all Business Associates. In other words, both direct subcontractors and downstream contractors must enter into Business Associate Agreements with any third party that provides services relating to the PHI unless the company falls into one of the narrow exceptions described above.

The Omnibus Rule also specifies that the Business Associate Agreement must contain certain terms requiring Business Associates to do, without limitation, the following: (a) comply with the security rule; (b) report breaches of PHI to the Covered Entity; (c) ensure that downstream subcontractors adhere to terms identical to that of the direct subcontractor; and (d) comply with applicable privacy rule requirements.

4. **Consent Required to Sell PHI and to Use and Disclose PHI for Marketing Purposes**

Under the Omnibus Rule, Covered Entities and Business Associates may not directly or indirectly sell PHI without obtaining individuals' express consent that the company may receive remuneration from the sale of the individual's PHI. There are a few exceptions to this requirement, including without limitation: (a) public health purposes; (b) treatment and payment purposes; (c) certain research purposes; and (d) legal requirements.

Covered Entities and Business Associates are still required to obtain individuals' authorization to disclose their PHI for marketing purposes under the Omnibus Rule, but the Omnibus Rule narrowed the definition of "marketing," so that it does not include the following as long as no payment is received from or on behalf of a third party whose products or services are being described: (a) refill reminders; and (b) communications for treatment and health care operations purposes.

5. **More Stringent Data Breach Notification Requirements**

Prior to enactment of the Omnibus Rule, a breach of PHI was defined as a use or disclosure that caused a "significant risk of financial, reputational, or other harm." This definition permitted companies to contemplate whether a data breach caused harm to the impacted individual. (For example, disclosing that a patient has the flu does not likely pose significant harm and therefore not require notification, but disclosing a patient's HIV status may pose significant harm and therefore require notification.). Now, a breach of PHI is defined to be an impermissible use of disclosure of PHI unless the Covered Entity or Business Associate can demonstrate there is a low probability that PHI has been compromised (which is difficult to establish). This change means that if a Covered Entity or Business Associate has a breach, it is more likely that the company will have to send out a breach notice.

6. **Application of Enforcement Provisions to Business Associates**

The Omnibus Rule specifies all Business Associates are now subject to compliance and enforcement by Health and Human Services ("**HHS**"). This means: (a) HHS may now directly receive and investigate complaints relating to Business Associates' compliance with HIPAA and the Omnibus Rule; and (b) HHS may impose monetary penalties against Business Associates.

7. **Updated Factors for Imposing Civil Monetary Penalties; Amount of Penalties Remains the Same**

The Omnibus Rule updates the factors HHS considers when determining the amount of a civil monetary penalty. The penalties are tiered and are dependent upon the Covered Entity's or Business Associate's knowledge and the willfulness of the breach. Generally, the factors HHS considers include without limitation: (a) the nature and extent of the violation; (b) the harm resulting from the violation (i.e., whether the violation caused physical, financial or reputational harm, prevented an individual from obtaining health care and past history of compliance); (c) the number of impacted individuals; and (d) the time period during which the violation occurred.

The Omnibus Rule does not modify civil monetary penalties. Tiered penalties still range from $100 for each violation, not to exceed $25,000 to $50,000 for each violation, not to exceed $1,500,000.

## B. Does Your Company Have to Comply with HIPAA and the Omnibus Rule?

Covered Entities and Business Associates that complied with HIPAA prior to March 26, 2013 must comply with the Omnibus Rule, and they should review their policies and practices to confirm they comply with the new Omnibus Rule. Downstream service providers that must comply with HIPAA and the Omnibus Rule as a result of the expanded definition of Business Associate under the Omnibus Rule must come into compliance by the dates set forth above.

## C. What Do Covered Entities and Business Associates Have to Do to Comply with HIPAA and the Omnibus Rule?

Below is a list of steps to take to become compliant with HIPAA and the Omnibus Rule. This list is not all-inclusive, and the steps a Covered Entity or Business Associate must take to become compliant will differ depending on each company's business practices and goals.

### 1. Review and Revise / Establish Policies and Procedures to Comply with the Security Rule—Establishing and Implementing Administrative, Physical and Technical Safeguards

Covered Entities and Business Associates (including both direct and downstream subcontractors) must have appropriate administrative, physical and technical safeguards in place, including without limitation: (a) establishing and implementing required security policies and procedures; (b) implementing technical security measures and facility access controls; (c) conducting regular audits and risk analyses; and (d) designating a security official and conducting company-wide training programs.

### 2. Review and Revise / Establish Policies and Procedures to Comply with the Privacy Rule

a. *Restrict Access to PHI*

Covered Entities and Business Associates (including both direct and downstream subcontractors) must comply with HIPAA's privacy rule which requires, without limitation: (i) limiting disclosure and use of PHI to the minimum number of third parties; (ii) requiring third parties receiving PHI and their subcontractors to enter legally-compliant business associate agreements (as applicable); (iii) maintaining compliance records; (iv) submitting reports to government regulatory authorities (as required); and (v) providing access to its covered entity or to the individual who is the subject of the PHI.

b. *Review and Revise/Develop Form Business Associate Agreement*

Review and revise or create Business Associate Agreements that comply with HIPAA and the new requirements of the Omnibus Rule, including without limitation, breach notification requirements. Confirm that the indemnification provisions adequately protect your company.

c. *Review and Revise/Develop Authorization Forms*

Review and revise or develop authorization forms that comply with the Omnibus Rule, including without limitation, authorization for the sale of PHI and the use and disclosure of PHI for marketing purposes.

d. *Update/Create a HIPAA-Compliant Privacy Notice*

Review your privacy notice or develop a privacy notice that complies with HIPAA and the Omnibus Rule, and distribute this revised or new notice as required by law. The privacy notice must, among other things, specify that any uses or disclosures of PHI other than those expressly permitted by the privacy rule will be made only with the written authorization of an individual, and addresses, without limitation, the following: (i) individuals' right to restrict disclosures of their PHI; (ii) the types of uses and disclosures of PHI that require individual authorization; (iii) an individual's right to opt out of certain disclosures of PHI; (iv) rights to notice in the event of a breach; (v) rights with respect to the use of genetic information (if applicable); (vi) informing individuals they may opt out of receiving fundraising communications (if applicable); and (vii) specifying that individuals must give written authorization for the covered entity to disclose uses and disclosures of PHI for marketing purposes and sale of PHI.

e. *Send a Security Breach Notice if PHI is Breached*

When a breach occurs, Covered Entities and Business Associates must notify HHS within certain time parameters. For breaches involving 500 or more people, the breach must be reported to HHS, and notice must be simultaneously provided to the impacted individuals. For breaches involving less than 500 people, the breach must be reported to HHS within sixty (60) days of the last day of the preceding calendar year in which the breach was discovered.

3. **Provide Training Sessions for Employees**

Conduct training sessions for your employees to inform them of your corporate policies and practices and what they must do to help your company be compliant.

4. **Consider State Law Issues**

HIPAA states that state law preempts HIPAA to the extent state law is more restrictive than HIPAA. Consider what state laws may apply to your company and whether they may preempt HIPAA's requirements.

*July 2013*

*About the author

Helen A. Christakos is Chair of Carr McClellan's IP, Privacy and Data Security group. She is an experienced business lawyer who represents clients in commercial transactions involving cutting edge intellectual property (IP) and technology issues. She advises companies ranging from global public companies to emerging start-up ventures in developing, licensing, selling, acquiring, protecting and commercially exploiting intellectual property and technology assets. She also devotes a significant portion of her practice to advising clients in a wide variety of industries on privacy, data security and ecommerce matters. Helen works with companies to assess their legal obligations and risks and helps design and implement plans for mitigating such risks. In addition to her law practice, Helen is Adjunct Professor at Santa Clara University School of Law, where she teaches J.D. and L.L.M. level classes in Technology and Intellectual Property Licensing. Helen's full bio is available at: http://

www.carrmcclellan.com/attorneys/helen-a-christakos/. If you have any questions about whether and how to comply with HIPAA and the new Omnibus Rule, please contact Helen at: hchristakos@carr-mcclellan.com.

This article is offered only for general informational and educational purposes. It is not offered as and does not constitute legal advice or a legal opinion. You should not act or rely on any information contained in this article without first seeking the advice of an attorney. This article does not and will not create any attorney-client or confidential relationship with Helen A. Christakos, Carr McClellan Ingersoll Thompson and Horn, LLP or any of its other attorneys.

# Chapter 19

## Avoiding Holiday Liability for Employers

by Stephanie Leach*

'Tis the season to be jolly. However, while you are enjoying the holiday cheer and a cup of hot chocolate, don't forget to take a moment to assess the potential legal liability that this holiday season may bring. Seemingly common scenarios can raise complex legal issues and, if they are not handled properly, can result in serious legal consequences.

It is important for employers to consider the variety of issues that may need to be addressed this holiday season, such as what sort of seasonal and holiday decorating will be permitted, how to address requests from employees to take time off work for religious observance, and what steps will be taken to reduce incidents and liability at company holiday parties. While employers do not need to avoid celebrating the holidays altogether, preventive planning can go a long way toward avoiding holiday problems.

### Holiday Decorations

The most important thing to remember is that an employer cannot treat persons of different religions differently. This basic premise should not be forgotten when dealing with holiday decorations. Employers may choose to limit the extent that holiday decorations are permitted in the workplace in certain instances; however, this limitation must be uniformly applied to all individuals and their respective religions.

Many employers prefer to decorate the office with non-religious decorations, such as winter/snow scenes, candy canes and strings of lights. Each year sparks a new debate as to whether a Christmas tree is considered religious. The U.S. Equal Employment Opportunity Commission has acknowledged the U.S. Supreme Court's determination that wreaths and Christmas trees are considered "secular" symbols. Therefore, employers may hang otherwise non-religious wreaths around the office or have a tree in the building lobby, even if an employee objects to such decorations.

The best practice for employers is to be sensitive to the diversity of the workplace and to not support or appear to support one religion over another.

**Holiday Religious Accommodations**

Title VII of the Civil Rights Act requires an employer to reasonably accommodate an employee's religious observances, practices and beliefs, as long as it can do so without undue hardship on the employer's business operations.

An employee's religious beliefs do not have to be part of a widely recognized faith in order to qualify for legal protection. Religion includes not only traditional, organized religions, but also religious beliefs that are new, uncommon, not part of a formal church or sect, only subscribed to by a small number of people, or that seem illogical or unreasonable to others. Err on the side of caution and do not jump to any conclusions that any given set of beliefs and practices, no matter how unusual, are not religious. If you are in doubt as to whether your employee's professed religious beliefs are subject to protection, it is wise to consult an attorney.

If an employer is going to deny a religious accommodation, it must be clear that such an accommodation requires more than ordinary administrative costs, diminishes efficiency in other jobs, infringes on other employees' job rights or benefits, impairs workplace safety, causes co-workers to carry the accommodated employee's share of potentially hazardous or burdensome work, or conflicts with other laws or regulations.

Thus, a request by a Jewish employee for a single day off on Hanukkah because his religious beliefs forbid working that day, or a request by a Christian employee for the last shift off on Christmas Eve because his religious beliefs require attendance at a Christmas Eve service are usually reasonable and the employer should attempt to accommodate these types of requests. Other types of religious accommodations include modifications of dressing and grooming standards, changes of policies regarding the use of the employer's facilities for religious purposes and permitting religious expressions in the workplace.

**Holiday Gift Exchanges**

Employers have a duty to maintain a harassment-free workplace under Title VII. If employees participate in holiday gift exchanges, employers should make clear that gifts should be respectful and appropriate for the workplace. For example, employees should not be permitted to exchange materials containing graphic lyrics or content, or holiday cards of an adult nature. While one employee may find such gifts humorous, another employee may take offense, especially if the gift is presented in a room full of co-workers and strangers.

**Holiday Parties**

Holiday parties should be unforgettable because of the festivities and fun, not because of the legal consequences that follow. Employers should consider the following holiday party best practices to protect themselves and their employees:

- Avoid using religious terms when describing office celebrations. Rather than referring to a party as a "Christmas party," it should be referred to as a "holiday party" or "annual celebration."
- Holiday parties often present situations for unwanted sexual overtures that could also lead to complaints of sexual harassment. Employers have a legal duty to prevent harassment at holiday parties, just like they have a legal duty to prevent harassment in the office. Therefore, publish or re-publish the company's sexual harassment policy before holiday parties take place. Remind employees that holiday festivities do not offer an excuse for violating a sexual harassment policy. If a company does not have a written policy, this would be a good time to implement one. In addition, given the proliferation of iPads and other technology devices, employers should be aware of, and take immediate action to prevent, any "techno harassment" at holiday parties and in the office.
- If alcohol is served, keep consumption in check. Limiting access

to alcohol by placing restrictions on the type served, the time available (such as by closing the bar well before the party ends) or the number of drinks served (such as through drink tickets) may reduce the possibility that employees will drink to excess. Providing food is also a good idea, as it typically slows the absorption of alcohol into the bloodstream. Providing plenty of non-alcoholic beverages is also a wise choice.

- Hire professional bartenders and require IDs from guests who do not appear to be 21 years of age or older. Ask the bartenders to keep their eyes open for obviously-intoxicated employees.
- Arrange designated drivers or cabs to ensure that all persons have a safe way to get home. Consider offering incentives to employees who offer to be designated drivers and/or pre-paid cab vouchers to employees.
- Make clear that employee attendance at the holiday party is voluntary and that employees are not required to attend.
- Invite spouses, significant others, families and important clients. Inviting employees' families and the company's important clients and others with whom the company conducts business can change the atmosphere of a company party and discourage inappropriate behavior.
- The time and place of the party will go a long way toward setting the tone, and picking the right ones can help eliminate problematic behaviors. A daytime event is far less likely to result in excessive drinking, or otherwise result in employees behaving inappropriately. Additionally, an event on a weekday, when employees know they have to work the next day, is likely to be more tame than one on a weekend. As far as location goes, if alcohol is being served at the party, the employer is better off hosting an event offsite.
- Most importantly, if there is a problem—deal with it promptly! Every act of sexual harassment—whether by a co-worker, client or supervisor—should be taken seriously. Prompt action designed to stop any further harassment not only demonstrates that the employer does not condone such behavior, but may prevent certain behavior from being imputed to the employer. Also, a record of consistent and effective response to incidents is important be-

cause the employer's entire record of dealing with such matters is considered when evaluating liability.

**Conclusion**

When getting ready for the holidays, don't forget the potential for liability, as compliance with the law takes no holiday. Have a safe and enjoyable holiday season and perhaps think twice before you hang mistletoe in the office.

*December 2013*

*About the author and firm

Stephanie R. Leach is an Arizona-based employment law attorney with the law firm Stephanie R. Leach, PLLC. Stephanie has years of extensive experience handling employment law issues and representing clients throughout Arizona and Florida.

Stephanie earned her undergraduate degree at the University of Florida (B.A., cum laude 1998) and her Juris Doctorate at the University of Miami School of Law (J.D., magna cum laude 2001) where she received the Order of the Coif. While a law student, Stephanie was an editor for the University of Miami Law Review, and tutored fellow law students as a Dean's Fellow.

Before forming Stephanie R. Leach, PLLC, Stephanie served as a law clerk to the Honorable Federico A. Moreno on the United States District Court for the Southern District of Florida and also for the Honorable Chief Justice Charles E. Jones of the Arizona Supreme Court. Stephanie also spent years working for large national law firms, representing employers in a wide range of matters.

Stephanie now continues to provide the same experienced, high quality representation to her clients that she did while practicing at large national law firms, but in a more cost efficient manner.

Stephanie is also actively involved in her community. She volunteers her time as a Judge Pro Tempore, and works as an adjunct professor at Arizona Summit Law School.

You can find more information about Stephanie and her firm at http://www.azemploymentattorney.com or via email at Stephanie@azemploymentattorney.com.

# Chapter 20

## Employee vs. Independent Contractor: What You Need to Know

by Roger Royse*

Employers take a risk when they classify someone performing services for them as an independent contractor instead of an employee. Because employers owe contractors far fewer obligations than employees, employers risk each of the following if a court determines that a misclassification occurred:

- Unpaid overtime
- Unpaid taxes
- Unprovided benefits
- A discrimination claim, or claims under other laws that protect employees but not contractors (i.e., the Family Medical Leave Act)

In determining whether a worker is an employee or an independent contractor, the IRS compares the degree of control exerted by the company to the degree of independence retained by the individual. Generally, the IRS examines this relationship in three ways:

1. Behavioral: Does the company control or have the right to control what the worker does and how the worker does his or her job?
2. Financial: Are the business aspects of the worker's job controlled by the payer? (These include things like how the worker is paid, whether expenses are reimbursed, who provides tools/supplies, etc.)
3. Type of Relationship: Are there written contracts or employee-type benefits (i.e., pension plan, insurance, vacation pay, etc.)? Will the relationship continue and is the work performed a key aspect of the business?

If you are considering classifying someone performing services for you as an independent contractor, your answers to these three questions will determine whether that individual is a bona fide contractor, or instead, is an employee. When in doubt, err on the side of caution. The government applies these tests aggressively to find employee status whenever it can. You should too, and the risks are too high to make a mistake.

## A. Hire a Contractor or an Employee?

Independent contractors and employees are not the same, and it's important to understand the difference. Knowing this distinction will help you determine what your first hiring move will be and affect how you withhold a variety of taxes and avoid costly legal consequences.

## B. What Is the Difference?

**An Independent Contractor:**

- Operates under a business name
- Has his/her own employees
- Maintains a separate business checking account
- Advertises his/her business' services
- Invoices for work completed
- Has more than one client
- Has own tools and sets own hours
- Keeps business records

**An Employee:**

- Performs duties dictated or controlled by others
- Is given training for work to be done
- Works for only one employer

Many small businesses rely on independent contractors for their staffing needs. There are many benefits to using contractors over hiring employees:

- Savings in labor costs
- Reduced liability
- Flexibility in hiring and firing

## C. Why Does It Matter?

Misclassification of an individual as an independent contractor may have a number of costly legal consequences. If your independent contractor is discovered to meet the legal definition of an employee, you may be required to:

- Reimburse them for wages you should have paid them under the Fair Labor Standards Act, including overtime and minimum wage
- Pay back taxes and penalties for federal and state income taxes, Social Security, Medicare and Unemployment Insurance
- Pay any misclassified injured employees workers' compensation benefits
- Provide employee benefits, including health insurance, retirement, etc.

## D. Tax Requirements

Visit the IRS Independent Contractor or Employee Guide to learn about the tax implications of either scenario, download and fill out a form to have the IRS officially determine your workers' status, and find other related resources.

## E. Employment Information

There is no single test for determining if an individual is an independent contractor or an employee under the Fair Labor Standards Act. However, the following guidelines should be taken into account:

1. The extent to which the services rendered are an integral part of the principal's business
2. The permanency of the relationship
3. The amount of the alleged contractor's investment in facilities and equipment
4. The nature and degree of control by the principal
5. The alleged contractor's opportunities for profit and loss
6. The amount of initiative, judgment, or foresight in open market competition with others that is required for the success of the claimed independent contractor

7. The degree of independent business organization and operation

Whether a person is an independent contractor or an employee generally depends on the amount of control exercised by the employer over the work being done. Read Equal Employment Opportunity Laws—Who's Covered? for more information on how to determine whether a person is an independent contractor or an employee, and which are covered under federal laws. If there is a serious concern as to whether you should classify an individual as an employee or independent contractor you may use Form SS-8 to ask the IRS to give its opinion.

**F. State Law**

The IRS, Department of Labor and many state agencies are taking aim at businesses using independent contractors. Why? Paying an independent contractor means no wage withholding, no employment taxes, no unemployment insurance, no workers' compensation, and no liability for pensions and fringe benefits. Even the red tape of nondiscrimination rules goes out the window.

When you look at the advantages of using independent contractors and at the amorphous question of who qualifies, it is clear why some businesses push the envelope. With tax revenues everywhere suffering, enforcement takes a front seat. Besides enforcing existing laws, new laws have been implemented to further punish wrongdoers. For example, California has passed legislation to increase the stakes:

- California's Labor and Workforce Development Agency can fine you for "willfully misclassifying" an employee from $5,000 to $15,000 per violation.
- The penalty goes up to $25,000 per violation if you commit a "pattern and practice" of "willfully misclassifying" workers.
- There is joint and several liability for consultants (but excluding practicing lawyers) who advise employers on such independent contractor engagements.
- It is unlawful to charge misclassified independent contractors any fee or take deductions from the compensation paid to them. Companies cannot deduct fees for goods, materials, space rental,

services, government licenses, repairs, etc. provided to contractors who are reclassified.

These penalties ***are in addition*** to existing penalties for misclassifying contractors. California's Labor Commissioner can enforce the law, but Private Attorney General Act lawsuits also seem to be allowed. Also, if a business has willfully misclassified an independent contractor, a prominent public notice must be posted for one year on a website or worksite reciting the misclassification.

*July 2013*

*About the author and firm

The original version of this article contained a section on California law relating to independent contractors. To access the complete article, visit http://rroyselaw.com/employee-vs-independent-contractor-what-you-need-to-know-2/.

Roger Royse is the Founder of Royse Law Firm, PC, and works with businesses ranging from newly formed startups to publicly traded multinationals in a variety of industries including technology, entertainment, real estate, sports, and agri-business. Roger is the author of Dead on Arrival: How to Avoid the Legal Mistakes that Could Kill Your Startup and has been an adjunct Professor of Taxation at Golden Gate University. Roger was awarded the 2012 San Francisco Bay Area Chapter Man of the Year in recognition of his charity work. Roger can be reached at rroyse @rroyselaw.com or (650) 813 9700.

Royse Law Firm, PC, (http://www.rroyselaw.com) provides sophisticated, yet affordable, legal services to growing companies, high net worth individuals and investment funds, with a focus on tax expertise that sets Royse Law Firm apart from other general business firms.

To ensure compliance with the requirements imposed by the IRS, we inform you that any tax advice contained herein is not intended or written to be used, and cannot be used, by any taxpayer for the purpose of (1) avoiding penalties under the Internal Revenue Code or (2) promoting, marketing or recommending to any other person any transaction or matter addressed herein.

The information in this article does not constitute legal advice and should not be used as a substitute for obtaining personal legal advice and consultation prior to making decisions regarding individual circumstances.

# Chapter 21

# New Developments Surrounding Lactation Discrimination

by Sarah Andrews and Sarah E. Bouchard*

When the Patient Protection and Affordable Care Act (ACA) was signed into law in 2010, we reported on a provision of the law that amended the Fair Labor Standards Act (FLSA) to require that covered employers offer unpaid lactation breaks to nursing mothers.[1] Employers should be aware of several new developments, which are summarized below.

<u>Sex Discrimination Claims Under Title VII</u>

On May 30, 2013 the U.S. Court of Appeals for the Fifth Circuit gave a boost to the Equal Employment Opportunity Commission's (EEOC's) position that lactation discrimination is a form of sex discrimination under Title VII by overturning a summary judgment victory for an employer in the district court. The decision represents a new direction for federal law and a potential new cause of action for employees denied the opportunity to express breast milk in the workplace.

In *EEOC v. Houston Funding*, an employee had a baby and then requested lactation space as part of negotiating her return to work. The employer rejected her request and suggested that the employee should continue to stay at home. She did stay home, and the company terminated her for job abandonment. The EEOC sued on the employee's behalf, and the U.S. District Court for the Southern District of Texas granted summary judgment to the employer, holding that the employee had no claim under Title VII because lactation was not a medical condition related to pregnancy.[2]

The EEOC appealed to the Fifth Circuit, which reversed, remanded, and ordered the employer to pay the plaintiff's costs for appeal.[3] The Fifth

Circuit engaged in a plain-meaning analysis of the statutorily undefined term "medical condition," noting that lactation is a physiological process caused by hormonal changes associated with pregnancy and childbirth. Ultimately, the court held, for the first time, that discrimination on the basis of lactation is pregnancy discrimination protected by Title VII.

Notably, the employee's request in Houston Funding was made before the enactment of section 207(r) of the FLSA, which requires that an employer provide a private space to express breast milk.

The Fifth Circuit's holding represents a new split in authority, as all other federal courts and many state courts that have considered lactation issues in the context of Title VII have previously maintained that lactation is not a medical condition related to pregnancy. Notably, the U.S. Court of the Appeals for the Eighth Circuit has an appeal pending on the same issue, and the district court in that case relied on the district court's now-reversed opinion in Houston Funding.

<u>Other Causes of Action Under the FLSA and ACA Amendments</u>

The litigation landscape under the FLSA remains murky because the lactation breaks provision in section 207(r) does not have an explicit cause of action for break time, only for wage violations. Accordingly, the first district court to decide an FLSA lactation break claim held, in an unpublished opinion, that a private cause of action might exist for retaliation claims related to lactation breaks under 29 U.S.C. § 215 but that enforcement actions for direct violations of the lactation breaks provision at section 207(r) were the province of the DOL.[4] However, a recent decision by the U.S. Court of Appeals for the Eleventh Circuit ruled on the merits of both a section 207(r) lactation breaks claim and a section 215 retaliation claim,[5] without addressing the issue of a private cause of action.

Additionally, there is another amendment to the FLSA that may affect litigation of the lactation breaks requirement. The ACA amended the FLSA to add 29 U.S.C. § 218c—the ACA's retaliation provisions. The text of this section purports to protect employees from discrimination or discharge for a long list of activities related to potential employer violations of any amendment created by the ACA. The lactation breaks provision of the FLSA is seemingly one such amendment, but no court has ruled as to whether section 218c creates a separate remedy for a lactation breaks violation.

What Employers Should Do

The risk associated with an employer's failure to accommodate a nursing employee is increasing. Recent litigation suggests that a noncompliant employer may face many different causes of action for such infractions, including (1) a cause of action under the sex discrimination provisions of Title VII, (2) a separate cause of action under the lactation provision of the FLSA, and (3) claims under the retaliation provisions of either law if the employee made a complaint followed by adverse employment action. That does not include the possible actions under a maze of state and local laws that protect similar conduct, especially as states begin to pass laws making it explicit that breastfeeding is protected conduct and/or that pregnancy-related conditions must be accommodated by employers.[6]

Ultimately, noncompliant employers could be forced to defend FLSA claims and weave through the EEOC administrative exhaustion requirements on the same set of facts. This compounds the risk of compensatory and punitive damages and fees as well as the risk of systemic litigation.

Appropriate planning can help mitigate this risk, however. Employers should review their policies to ensure that they are compliant with federal and relevant state law protections, which can be more expansive than the federal requirement. The DOL has reported that, for the first two years the lactation breaks amendment to the FLSA was in effect, it conducted 54 investigations and found 36 violations, the great majority of which related to employers' failure to provide a private space for lactation breaks. In addition to preparing to make appropriate spaces available, employers may benefit from offering training aimed at creating a culture friendly to nursing mothers. At least one case and one $200,000 settlement of a complaint involved lactating employees alleging that they were subjected to video surveillance while pumping. In the end, as case law continues to emerge in this area, it is clear that employers can decrease risk by establishing open lines of communication with employees to develop practical solutions to both issues of legal compliance and the employer's business needs.

Additionally, employers should carefully consider whether lactation breaks should be paid or unpaid. Although nonexempt employees are only entitled to unpaid lactation break time, the DOL has been clear that, when an employer offers compensated break time (typically 20 minutes or less), the employer must pay an employee who uses that time to express milk in the same manner as other employees and that an employee must be completely relieved from duty before a break can be unpaid.[7] Further, employers should be mindful that, although exempt employees are not technically covered by the lactation protections in section 207(r),[8] employers may lose the right to claim that an employee is exempt by engaging in an actual practice of improper deductions from salary[9] and should, therefore, consider adopting a universal lactation break program.

*June 2013*

*About the authors



Sarah Andrews is an associate in Morgan Lewis's Labor and Employment Practice. You can view her biography and contact information at http://www.morganlewis.com/bios/sarahandrews. Sarah E. Bouchard is a partner in Morgan Lewis's Labor and Employment Practice and a co-leader of the Sarbanes-Oxley subpractice. You can view her biography and contact information at http://www.morganlewis.com/bios/sbouchard.



Endnotes

1. For more information on unpaid lactation breaks, see our April 7, 2010 LawFlash, "Healthcare Reform Law Requires Reasonable Break Times and Locations for Nursing Mothers," available at http://www.morganlewis.com/pubs/WashGRPP_NursingMothers_LF_07apr10. For an analysis of the requirements of the law, the informal guidance published by the Department of Labor (DOL), analogous and related state lactation leave and breastfeeding laws, and counseling notes for employers, see our article, "Lactation Breaks

in the Workplace: What Employers Need to Know About the Nursing Mothers Amendment to the FLSA," available at http://www.morganlewis.com/pubs/Andrews_LactationBreaks_Fall2012.pdf.

2. *EEOC v. Houston Funding II, Ltd.*, No. H-11-2442, 2012 WL 739494, at *1-2 (S.D. Tex. Feb. 2, 2012) (holding that all pregnancy-related medical conditions "ended" the day the employee gave birth).

3. *EEOC v. Houston Funding II, Ltd.*, --- F.3d ----, 2013 WL 2360114, at *3 (5th Cir. May 30, 2013). At the time of publication, the employer had not filed a motion for rehearing.

4. *Salz v. Casey's Mktg. Co.*, No. 11-CV-3055-DEO, 2012 WL 2952998, at *7 (N.D. Iowa July 19, 2012).

5. *Miller v. Roche Sur. & Cas. Co.*, 502 F. App'x 891 (11th Cir. 2012).

6. For more information, see our December 28, 2012 LawFlash, "New California Disability Regulations to Become Effective December 30," available at http://www.morganlewis.com/pubs/LEPG_LF_NewCAPregnancyRelatedDisabilityRegulations_28dec12, and our October 3, 2012 LawFlash, "Another New Wave of Employment Laws in California," available at http://www.morganlewis.com/pubs/LEPG_LF_NewCaliforniaLaborLaws_3oct12.

7. See DOL FAQs at http://www.dol.gov/whd/nursingmothers/faqBTNM.htm.

8. Exempt employees are, however, covered by many analogous state laws.

9. See DOL Fact Sheet 17g at http://www.dol.gov/whd/regs/compliance/fairpay/fs17g_salary.htm

# Chapter 22

# Obesity as a Disability Under the ADA: Is It More Likely Now Than Before?

by Cherie Blackburn*

In July, the American Medical Association (AMA) adopted a new policy that officially labels obesity as a disease, "requiring a range of medical interventions to advance obesity treatment and prevention." According to the AMA's Council on Science and Public Health, a "disease" is defined as having the following criteria: 1) an impairment of the normal functioning of some aspect of the body; 2) characteristic signs or symptoms; and 3) harm or morbidity.

The AMA's focus on obesity as a disease has centered on the question of whether obesity may be a disability under the Americans with Disabilities Act (ADA). The definition of disability under the ADA is:

- A physical or mental impairment that substantially limits one or more major life activities;
- A record of such an impairment; or
- Being regarded as having such an impairment.

While the ADA does not identify obesity as a disability, several events in recent years—including the AMA's July policy declaration—make it more likely that obesity, and certainly morbid obesity, will be treated as a disability under the ADA.

**2008: Congress Broadens Definition of "Disability"**

In 2008, Congress enacted the American with Disabilities Act Amendments Act (ADAAA). In doing so, it declared its intent that the definition of "disability" be construed broadly to afford greater protection to employees. Although the ADAAA does not change the definition of disability, it broadens the term by modifying key language within that definition. Following enactment of the ADAAA, it is more likely that an individual's physical or mental impairment will be considered a "disability" under the ADA.

Prior to enactment of the ADAAA, the Equal Employment Opportunity Commission (EEOC) took the position that severe or morbid obesity—though not necessarily obesity itself—was an impairment. The EEOC's Interpretive Guidance, which is incorporated into the federal regulations on the ADA, concluded, prior to the ADAAA, that "except in rare circumstances, obesity is not considered a disabling impairment." However, when the 2011 Interpretive Guidance was published in the Code of Federal Regulations, this language was omitted, suggesting that the EEOC no longer considers obesity to be a disability only "in rare circumstances."

**2012: EEOC Settles Two Cases That Focused on Obesity as a Disability**

In 2012, the EEOC settled two cases in which it alleged discrimination based on an employee's obesity.

In the first, EEOC v. Resources for Human Development, Inc., the commission brought suit on behalf of the estate of Lisa Harrison, a former employee of the company, alleging that RHD violated the ADA in terminating her because she was obese and was regarded as disabled. Harrison weighed more than 400 pounds when she was hired and weighed 527 pounds when she was terminated eight years later. According to the EEOC, she received "excellent" ratings in her performance evaluations. Harrison died two years after her termination as a result of "morbid obesity."

The District Court for the Eastern District of Louisiana ruled that severe obesity—defined as a body weight of more than 100 percent over the norm—is an impairment. Relying on the EEOC's Interpretive Guidance, the court found that if an individual is severely obese, there is no requirement that the obesity be based on a physiological impairment. Thus, Harrison qualified as disabled under the ADA. The parties settled the case for $125,000 following the District Court's ruling.

In the second case, EEOC v. BAE Systems Tactical Vehicle Systems, LP, the EEOC filed suit in a Texas district court alleging that BAE fired its employee, Ronald Kratz, because of his disability, morbid obesity, and because it regarded him as disabled. Kratz was hired by BAE in 1994. In 2009, he was informed that BAE felt he could no longer perform his job duties because of his weight. According to Kratz, he asked whether he could be transferred to a different position or be provided with other reasonable accommodations, and BAE refused. At the time he was terminated, Kratz weighed 680 pounds. In July 2012, BAE entered into a settlement with the EEOC that required the company to pay $55,000 to Kratz and to provide disability discrimination training to its employees.

In a press release detailing the BAE settlement, senior EEOC trial attorney Kathy Boutchee stated that the ADA "protects morbidly obese employees and applicants from being subjected to discrimination because of their obesity." Boutchee explained:

> So long as an employee can perform the essential job duties of a position, with or without reasonable accommodation, the employee should be allowed to work on the same basis as any non-obese employee. Employers cannot fire disabled employees based on perceptions and prejudice.

Boutchee's statement clarified the EEOC's position that morbid obesity, by itself and without some additional underlying physiological disorder, may constitute a disability under the ADA.

**Will Courts Routinely Consider Obesity a Disability Under ADA?**

With the AMA's designation of disability as a disease, employers should understand that it may be only a matter of time before the courts routinely consider obesity as a disability under the ADA. Obesity for adults is defined by looking at a person's BMI, which is a measure of body fat based on weight and height. An individual with a BMI of 30 or higher is considered obese.

According to the Centers for Disease Control and Prevention (CDC), the U.S. obesity rate increased almost 50 percent between 1997 and 2012. Today, more than one-third of adults in the United States—35.7 percent—are considered obese. Based on the statistical information the CDC maintains, every state in the nation had a prevalence of obesity at 20 percent or more in 2012, and 13 of these states—including South Carolina and several others in the South—had a prevalence of 30 percent or more.

## Considerations For Employers

Before making employment decisions that adversely affect employees who may be obese or morbidly obese, employers should consider whether the decision would be different if the employee were considered disabled under the ADA. For example, is there an accommodation that would allow the employee to perform the essential functions of his or her job and eliminate the need for the adverse action?

In addition, employers need to caution their supervisory and management-level employees not to regard an individual as disabled simply because he or she is overweight. Taking adverse action against the employee because the employee is overweight may violate the ADA's prohibition against discriminating against an individual because he or she is regarded as disabled, even if the person is not disabled. Notably, the ADAAA eliminated the requirement that an employee establish that the employer perceived him or her to be substantially limited in a major life activity. Now, the employee need only demonstrate that the employer took an adverse action based on the employee's actual or perceived physical or mental impairment.

It remains to be seen whether the AMA's recent designation of obesity as a disease will have an effect on court decisions addressing obesity and the ADA. It does appear, however, particularly given the EEOC's position on this issue, that courts will look at the issue more closely and may not readily rule out obesity as a disability.

*September 2013*

*About the author and firm

Cherie Blackburn is a partner with Nexsen Pruet, LLC, in the firm's Charleston, South Carolina office. She has been representing companies in employment lawsuits in state and federal court for over 20 years.

Nexsen Pruet is a full-service firm with more than 190 attorneys practicing in eight offices across South Carolina and North Carolina. Ms. Blackburn may be reached at cblackburn@nexsenpruet.com or 843-720-1728. The information in this article does not constitute legal advice.

# Chapter 23

## "You Can't Fire Me For That—I Was Off Duty!"

by Jeffrey A. Dretler*

Employers learned long ago that it's wise to establish written policies which set forth the standards of conduct expected of their employees. These employers also know that the policies may not simply sit on a shelf (or on an intranet), but must be monitored and enforced in order to remain effective tools for encouraging or prohibiting certain behavior. But can you rely on your policies to discipline or terminate employees for engaging in legal conduct which occurred off-duty, especially if the conduct also occurred off-premises, and did not negatively impact the employee's performance of his or her duties or your business?

While you are probably familiar with laws which protect an employee's right to engage in what is sometimes referred to as "protected conduct" (e.g., making a charge of discrimination, complaining of wage and hour violations, whistleblowing, filing a workers' compensation claim, requesting reasonable accommodation of a disability, engaging in concerted union activity as defined in the NLRA) without fear of retaliation, other lawful activities may also be deemed "protected" by certain statutes, although not always without limitation. The following, which is by no means an exhaustive list, are some examples of off-duty conduct which may or may not be grounds for discipline or termination, depending on the state and the circumstances.

### Medical Marijuana

In *Roe v. Teletech Customer Care Management* (2011), an applicant for a position as a customer-service representative for a telesales company was offered employment conditioned on her passing the company's reference and background checks and a drug screening policy. The applicant, who had already started attending training for the position, submitted to the drug screen, and tested positive for marijuana. The applicant informed the company that she suffered from debilitating migraine headaches and used medical marijuana at home, as prescribed by her doctor, which was legal under Washington's Medical Use of Marijuana Act (MUMA), and even offered to provide a doctor's note to prove it.

Unmoved, the company withdrew its offer of employment based on the applicant's failure to pass the drug screen, even though there was no evidence that the employee was under the influence of marijuana at work or that her work would have been affected in any way. The applicant sued, but to no avail. The Washington Supreme Court determined that MUMA, while providing an affirmative defense to criminal prosecution, did not create a private right of action for individuals to bring suit, nor did it establish a public policy which prohibited employers from refusing to hire applicants or discharging employees who legally used medical marijuana.

But if the same situation had arisen in Arizona it would have yielded a different result. Unlike the Washington state statute, Arizona's medical marijuana statute explicitly prohibits employers from discriminating against registered marijuana patients unless the employment of such patients would cause the employer to lose money or licensing under federal law (i.e., because medical marijuana use is not legal under federal law). Arizona does permit employers, however, to prohibit even registered users from possession of medical marijuana on company premises or from impairment while working. Rhode Island also prohibits employers from discriminating against medical marijuana users.

## Firearms

While most employers may prefer that employees not bring firearms onto company property, some states have laws which protect an employee's right to do so. For example, Florida expressly prohibits employers from asking employees about the presence of a firearm in a vehicle and from searching a private vehicle to determine if it contains a firearm. Similarly, Mississippi makes it unlawful for an employer to prohibit individuals from storing or transporting firearms in their own locked vehicles in company parking areas. A number of other states (including Arizona, Georgia, Idaho, Indiana, Kentucky, Louisiana, Maine, Minnesota, Mississippi, North Dakota, Oklahoma, Utah, Wisconsin) protect an employee's right, with some limitations, to possess a legal firearm on company premises.

**Tobacco**

In Massachusetts, a number of hospitals have established policies prohibiting smoking on company premises and some will even refuse to hire any candidate who tests positive for nicotine, on the theory that the hospital's mission to promote a healthy lifestyle is harmed by employees who act contrary to the hospital's message. Some employers in other industries have done the same.

In *Rodrigues v. EG Systems d/b/a/ Scotts Lawn Services* (2009), an applicant whose contingent offer of employment was withdrawn after he tested positive for nicotine, consistent with the company's policy not to employ smokers, brought suit against his employer claiming invasion of privacy and violation of ERISA. A federal court in Massachusetts dismissed the claim, reasoning that the employee had no privacy claim as it was no secret that he smoked, and had no ERISA claim as he was only a prospective employee and had no expectation of benefits under the company's ERISA plan.

Massachusetts has no state law which prohibits employers from establishing this kind of policy. But in many other regions of the country, company policies refusing to hire smokers would be expressly prohibited. For example, Connecticut, Washington D.C., Indiana, Kentucky, Louisiana, Maine, Mississippi, Missouri, New Hampshire, New Mexico, South Carolina, South Dakota, Tennessee, Virginia, West Virginia and Wyoming, among others, all have statutes protecting the rights of employees to smoke away from company premises.

**Other Lawful Protected Activity**

In addition to laws that protect specific types of off-duty conduct, some states have enacted laws which protect broad categories of off-duty conduct or require that an employer demonstrate some nexus between the employee's engagement in an activity and the employer's business before allowing the employer to take adverse action against the employee for engaging in the conduct.

In Colorado, for example, it is illegal for an employer to terminate an employee because that employee engaged in *any* lawful activity off the employer's premises during nonworking hours unless the restriction 1) relates to a bona fide occupational requirement or is reasonably and rationally related to the employee's employment activities and responsibilities; or 2) is necessary to avoid, or avoid the appearance of, a conflict of interest with any of the employee's responsibilities to the employer.

In Montana, an employer is prohibited from refusing to hire a job applicant or disciplining or discharging an employee for using "lawful consumable products" (such as tobacco or alcohol) if the products are used off the employer's premises outside of work hours, with certain exceptions for a bona fide occupational requirement or a conflict of interest, similar to Colorado's law.

In addition to the examples set forth above, a number of states also limit an employer's ability to use an applicant's or employee's credit history as grounds for employment decisions, and prohibit employers from requesting access to the social-media accounts of applicants or employees. Moreover, public employers are even more restricted than private employers in that certain conduct engaged in by public employees is constitutionally protected by the First Amendment (free speech).

**Unionized Workplaces**

In unionized settings, where employers are usually required to prove "just cause" for termination, it is important for employers to show not only a violation of a company policy and an absence of statutorily or other protected conduct, but the impact which the employee's conduct had on the employer's business.

In *Vista Nuevas Head Start* (2011), an arbitrator found that the employer, a Head Start program, had just cause to discharge a teacher for her Facebook page griping about her work, even though she posted comments off-duty, where her posts tended to undermine her working relationship with center administrator, classroom partners, and parents of children in classroom.

By contrast, in *L'Anse Creuse Public Schools* (2008), an arbitrator held that a school district did not have just cause to terminate a teacher, even after photos of the teacher engaged in sexually explicit activity turned up on the internet, because the activity occurred off-duty, off-premises, and the photos were taken and posted without the teacher's knowledge or permission.

**The Bottom Line**

As the above examples illustrate, employers must carefully analyze each situation before making the decision to refuse to hire a candidate or to discipline or terminate an employee for having engaged in lawful off-duty conduct, even if such conduct violates the employer's established policy.

*February 2014*

*<u>About the author and firm</u>

Jeffrey Dretler is a partner in the Boston office of Fisher & Phillips LLP (http://www.laborlawyers.com), a national labor and employment firm representing employers. Jeff regularly appears in state and federal courts and administrative agencies on behalf of clients in matters involving discrimination, harassment, wrongful termination, retaliation, civil rights, and wage and hour issues. He also provides counsel on reasonable accommodation, independent contractor law, workplace investigations, the Family and Medical Leave Act, and both drafts and negotiates employment agreements, noncompetition agreements and severance agreements. Jeff's clients span a broad range of industries with a particular focus on health care, media, and hospitality. Jeff is active in the American Bar Association's Section of Labor and Employment Law, where he currently serves as the Management Co-Chair of both its Leadership Development Program committee and the Employment At Will subcommittee of its Employment Rights and Responsibilities committee. Jeff earned his B.A. from Northwestern University in Evanston, Illinois and his J.D. from Northeastern University School of Law in Boston, Massachusetts. Immediately after law school, Jeff served as law clerk to the Honorable William G. Young of the U.S. District Court for the District of Massachusetts. Jeff has been recognized as a "Super

Lawyer" for employment litigation defense in 2012 and 2013. Jeff can be reached at jdretler@laborlawyers.com or 617-532-9322.

# Chapter 24

# Protecting Your Business with Strong Operational Privacy Controls

by Paul Glist, Christin S. McMeley and Daniel P. Reing*

For decades basic requirements to secure business records have been rooted in various legal silos, from corporate governance to rules of evidence to the discrete privacy rules that govern select technologies. Today, however, data security is becoming an integral part of how government authorities, the press, and the public judge how well companies protect personal privacy—and whether they can be trusted to do so without the need for even more intrusive mandatory laws and regulations. Incorporating robust operational controls over how personally identifiable information (PII) is secured, and thus how consumers' privacy is maintained, will be key to an organization's ability to avoid future enforcement actions, comply with looming legislative or regulatory action, and sustain consumer confidence.

**Federal and State Direction**

This expanded focus on what and how information must be secured to protect privacy is evident from increased activity at both the federal and state levels.

The FTC, for example, changed the privacy debate in its 2012 white paper entitled Protecting Consumer Privacy in an Era of Rapid Change: Recommendations for Businesses and Policymakers. Before that white paper, information was either PII or not; consumers suffered tangible harm from intrusion or they did not. After the white paper, the lines grew blurred: information purged of name and address could still be "personal," and consumer fears could be cognizable in law, even if no tangible harm was suffered. In the more subtle new world, how a company secures and handles information may very well determine whether "personal" information has been shown enough respect to dissipate "harmful" fears and meet the rising expectations for privacy protection.

The FTC has taken this approach on the road. In one of the few areas where it has rulemaking authority, it added security obligations to the Children's Online Privacy Protection Act ("COPPA"). Where it does not have rulemaking authority, it has taken enforcement action against companies of various sizes and in various industries for not delivering consumers promised or "reasonable and appropriate" security—whether or not any consumer suffered direct harm—especially when such security defenses were publicly available at low or no cost. The vast majority of these target companies—including Facebook, Google, and most recently TRENDnet—reach settlements with the FTC that include establishing comprehensive security programs with robust operational controls. Companies like Wyndham Hotels and LabMD are challenging the FTC's authority to enforce what they call "arbitrary" security standards that have not been formally promulgated. But the fact remains that the FTC continues to bring enforcement actions; privacy issues continue to dominate discussions in the legislative, regulatory and public arenas; and those discussions increasingly call for operational controls to ensure the security of information, and thereby ensure privacy compliance.

The Department of Health and Human Services (HHS) has also been busy bringing enforcement actions against companies that have failed to take proper measures to secure patients' personal health information (PHI). In August, HHS published a $1.2 million settlement with a company that failed to wipe PHI from the hard drive of a leased photocopier before turning it back in to the leasing company, a precaution that would be wise for any company handling PII.

Federal agencies are not alone. State legislatures and attorneys general have certainly not waited for the federal government to enact uniform legislation before taking on privacy and data security themselves. Many state data breach laws have built-in incentives to encrypt stored personal information. Massachusetts and Nevada have taken the direct route by imposing encryption and data security requirements, regardless of breach. Fourteen states currently require that data breach notifications be sent to the attorney general's office. Maryland Attorney General Doug Gansler made privacy a priority of the National Association of Attorneys General and a priority for Maryland. Numerous attorneys general have followed suit by creating Internet privacy units within their offices, claiming existing authority to treat data breaches or failure to meet privacy promises as unfair and deceptive trade practices under state law, and often coordinating their privacy enforcement. Gansler and Connecticut's Attorney General George Jepsen met Living Social's recent breach notice with lengthy and detailed requests for additional information. Jepsen's Privacy Task Force teamed up with California Attorney General Kamala Harris to investigate a breach of an online credit card security system and reached an August 29, 2013 settlement. Harris's Privacy Unit is aggressively pursuing privacy enforcement actions and seeking new enforcement hooks through state privacy legislation. Harris recently recommended that the state legislature require encryption for data in transit, and expand "personal information" to include online credentials such as email addresses or other usernames and the passwords that would permit access to an account. Nebraska and Pennsylvania statutes explicitly provide that it is an unfair business practice for a business to knowingly make a false or misleading statement in an online privacy policy.

**Self-Regulation and Multi-Stakeholder Collaboration**

In the face of the increased willingness by federal and state authorities to regulate and enforce privacy and security promises and protocols, active self-regulation and multi-stakeholder processes have become more important to demonstrate that industry understands the importance of keeping personal information secure.

Of course, security has long been a part of Fair Information Practice Principles (FIPPs), and any company that holds itself to FIPPs standards has long had security obligations. Under the White House privacy initiative and the Commerce Department "bill of rights," personal data (broadly defined) must be secured. But security has taken on new momentum in the many multi-stakeholder processes now underway. In the World Wide Web Consortium's (W3C) Do-Not-Track (DNT) process, the debate shifted away from a stark black and white world in which data was either personal or anonymous and consumers were either tracked or not tracked, and moved to a more nuanced acceptance of the controlled usage of information if permitted uses are delimited and security measures protect against unpermitted uses. The same approach—embedding data security principles as part of privacy protection frameworks—is part of NTIA's multi-stakeholder work on mobile privacy, and in NIST guidance on how to de-identify information. Various draft privacy bills echoed similar themes in prior Congresses—securing consumer information is necessary to ensure that consumers are protected in their privacy choices.

In attacking the problem of cybersecurity for critical infrastructure, NIST, with industry participation, is already paving a formal road for migrating from occasional efforts to secure data systems to systematic security built into company procedures and treating cybersecurity risk as a part of an organization's overall risk management portfolio. The draft NIST framework, although voluntary, paints a picture of what potential litigants may claim to be the *de facto* ***reasonable*** standard for cybersecurity. The current environment at both the state and federal levels suggests that similar standards may be imposed on companies' handling and securing of personal data.

All these trends point industry to adopt robust technical and organizational controls on data.

**What Do You Do?**

In this environment, it is worth asking yourself (and your legal, IT, engineering, product development, marketing, HR and finance departments) just how well you secure data that government authorities, the press, and the public may judge to be threateningly personal. It is not enough to assume that IT is "handling it." All departments need to partner with other groups in the organization who collect, access, store or use customer and employee information. What is "reasonable" will depend on the company's size, business and technological capabilities as well as the nature and amount of information it collects. But you should specifically ask:

- Who is responsible for your organization's security program?
- Have you identified your data assets and determined the need for protection as a result of legal requirements and business need?

- Do you run background checks on personnel who handle protected data?
- Do you have the paper trail of NDAs, records of access, retention policies and internal audits?
- Do you go beyond paper policies and train personnel who handle protected data? Do you periodically refresh and reinforce that training (e.g. implementing "pop-quizzes" or internal "spear-phishing" attempts)?
- Do you physically secure your computers and servers against unauthorized physical access?
- Do you restrict access to protected information to need-to-know personnel?
- Do you secure networked workstations and other devices with firewalls, password policies, and centralized patch management?
- Do you secure your network perimeter, limit remote access and maintain intrusion detection and response systems? Do you review the logs, monitor alarms, and respond accordingly?
- Do you protect data at rest and in transit?
- Do you periodically conduct risk assessments and test your network against penetration?
- Do you have policies, procedures, and teams in place to respond immediately to breach?
- Do you have contracts in place that commit service providers, vendors and other counterparties to security, limited data uses, audit and breach response, and indemnity?

Self-policing is also part of privacy by design—a concept endorsed and enforced by the FTC. You want to design privacy into your enterprise operations and audit your products and services before the Wall Street Journal or a regulator does it for you. Ideally, your organization accounts for privacy protections when designing products and services in the same way it accounts for components and costs. This way, you do not have to hold a launch or retrofit a product after the fact—or worse, after an enforcement action is brought. You internalize privacy in your organization, giving privacy and security responsibilities to a CPO, CISO or other executive, with specific reporting, security, and accountability protocols. You prepare your executives for rapid response when they are called by reporters or summoned to the FTC or Capitol Hill. You know your FIPPs and how your technology addresses every element. You know the life of your data from birth to disposition, so that you will not be surprised when reporters come calling. When your products are created or supported by third parties, you ensure their compliance with your standards. Where possible, you tie the use of data to actual consumer benefits and you give some level of choice to consumers. When you self-regulate in a meaningful way, whether it is following third party guidelines or crafting protections appropriate to your particular company, you will not only protect personal data, you will promote and differentiate your brand as one that can be trusted, and you will protect your business.

Not long ago, C-level executives might have been skeptical about investing resources in privacy, but today, there are some pretty clear reasons for investing.

- First, the press or Capitol Hill can shut you down, as both did to NebuAd. Both expect privacy protections, whether or not they are "the law" or required by the opinion letter you have. The FTC is already treating conduct it deems offensive to those expectations as an unfair or deceptive act that it can punish without waiting for any new law—and state AGs are following suit. Your product needs to protect privacy, and not be seen as an affront to consumer or political expectations. At a minimum, respecting privacy is insurance.
- Second, responsible privacy policies can create trust, and trust is valued currency in the market and before government.
- Third, proactively adopting security measures can help you retain your freedom to innovate and change. Sooner or later, rules are coming—whether legislative or "voluntary" reasonableness standards. Self-regulation is far more flexible than legislation. What gets fixed into law creates design constraints that cannot keep up with technology. Self-regulatory principles can respect privacy but still adjust rapidly with innovation and changing consumer expectations.

All businesses have the opportunity today to protect privacy and to protect their own businesses with practical operational privacy controls that work—before enforcement actions, intrusive mandatory regulations, or a loss of consumer confidence leads to far more intrusive requirements.

*September 2013*

*<u>About the authors and firm</u>

Paul Glist and Christin S. McMeley are partners and Daniel P. Reing is a senior associate at Davis Wright Tremaine LLP, a full-service firm with approximately 500 lawyers in nine offices on the east and west coasts of the United States and in Shanghai. We are recognized for excellence in a broad number of areas, with 88 of our attorneys across 43 practice areas cited as leaders in their fields in the most recent Chambers USA guide, and over 140 of our attorneys across 46 practice areas included in the 2013 edition of "The Best Lawyers in America." The DWT Privacy and Security team provides solution-oriented legal services and strategic advice for in-house counsel who must contend with the often competing demands of risk management, time constraints, cost control, regulatory compliance, and brand protection. For more information about our Privacy and Security practice and team, please contact PaulGlist@dwt.com, ChristinMcMeley@dwt.com, or DanielReing@dwt.com or visit http://www.privsecblog.com. This article is not intended, nor should it be used, as a substitute for specific legal advice as legal counsel may only be given in response to inquiries regarding particular situations.

# Chapter 25

# Five Documents Sure to Appear in Your Lawsuit

by Mauro Ramirez*

Although simple and oftentimes overused, sports metaphors can provide insight into complicated topics. When it comes to employment litigation, cases often boil down to "blocking and tackling." In other words, the fundamental (but unglamorous) activities often make a far greater difference than sophisticated lawyering.

Employment litigation can easily prove both complicated and time consuming. Interpretations regarding legal concepts often evolve rapidly, based on court decisions, agency interpretations, or actions by Congress or state legislatures. And even though claims are based on these changing laws, basic documents created by an employer lie at the core of an employment dispute. In litigation, these documents can make the difference between success and failure.

**The Big Five**

Five key documents arise most frequently, especially in cases involving an alleged adverse employment action: the job description; the handbook; performance evaluations; disciplinary documents; and responses to administrative charges. They vary in importance depending on the claims asserted and the underlying issues, but they're almost always included among documents produced in employment litigation.

In fact, these documents are included in the "Pilot Project Regarding Initial Discovery Protocols For Employment Cases Alleging Adverse Action," which some Federal District Courts are already requiring. This program introduces pre-trial procedures aimed at encouraging efficient and less costly discovery. The Pilot Project accepts that there is a core set of documentation exchanged in litigation and asks that a mandatory list of documents be exchanged even without a request by the employee's counsel.

Included in the mandatory list are the following: 1) "Job description(s) for the position(s) that the plaintiff held"; 2) "Workplace policies relevant to the adverse action in effect at the time of the adverse action" and "The table of contents and index of any employee handbook..."; 3) "The plaintiff's performance evaluations..."; 4) "The plaintiff's...formal discipline" and "Documents concerning the...termination...of the employment relationship at issue in this lawsuit"; and 5) "Responses to...administrative charges and complaint by the plaintiff that rely upon any of the same factual allegations or claims as those at issue in this lawsuit."

Absent the Pilot Project, any diligent plaintiff's attorney will surely request these documents. So, knowing that these documents will most certainly be read by an employee's lawyer, a judge, or a jury—why not make certain that they are going to help make a potential litigation successful?

Like tackling and blocking in football, these documents are fundamental but not glamorous—generally requiring meticulous drafting or frequent revision. The impact that they make in litigation, however, can lead directly to success or defeat. Let's take a closer look at each.

**Job Descriptions**

Of the five documents, job descriptions are often the most overlooked. With positions often evolving or with companies changing structures, it can be difficult to keep up with an employee's core duties and functions.

But a fundamental question in litigation is going to be, "What did this person do?" Although a supervisor can provide this information through testimony at a later time, it is always best to have a contemporaneous document that clearly sets out both the employee's job duties and expectations.

This information can prove important for various reasons. With respect to claims for failing to either hire or promote an employee, the duties that the employer felt the applicant could not successfully accomplish serve as a central issue. The essential functions of a job are an important aspect in many litigations involving the Americans with Disabilities Act.

Although not determinative, the job description helps in establishing duties or responsibilities in misclassification claims under the Fair Labor Standards Act. In unlawful discrimination or retaliation claims where an employer terminated an employee because of failure to properly execute job duties, it's helpful to have documentation establishing that the employee was indeed the one responsible for fulfilling the duties in question.

Let's say you fire a salesperson for failing to achieve consistently positive customer satisfaction scores. It is helpful in subsequent litigation to use the job description as a basic document to establish that you expected the employee to achieve such scores, and that the employee understood the expectation. Although such an expectation may appear obvious to a manager or human resources representative, a third-party who later evaluates the claim may not be familiar with your business or expectations.

**Handbooks**

Handbooks serve a critical role in any place of employment since they set out basic policies for employees. Unfortunately, however, handbooks can negatively impact employment litigation as much as they can help support important arguments.

Handbooks often serve as the document establishing that the employer has policies prohibiting the conduct the employee complains about, such as policies on equal employment opportunities, medical leave, and requesting accommodations. Clear policies regarding reporting potential harassment or discrimination underpin important legal defenses—especially when employees fail to use reporting avenues.

But a handbook that fails to provide succinct and relevant policies does not serve as good guidance for employees; it even poses a danger during potential litigation. This most often occurs where handbook policies set out intentions or expectations that are not consistently applied or were not applied properly in the events resulting in the lawsuit. This could involve policies related to attendance, tardiness, or general expectations regarding behavior.

Of course, policies should be updated and revised regularly. Even if there is no discriminatory motive, a manager's reliance on an outdated—or unlawful—policy will undoubtedly assist an employee in mounting a challenging case. For example, a manager may terminate or discipline an employee based on a policy that prohibits employees from discussing their pay with coworkers. In a subsequent Title VII litigation, the manager may not have intended to discriminate against the employee based on race or gender, but the policy applied violates the National Labor Relations Act. Even though the NLRA is not at issue in the litigation, it still creates an uncomfortable circumstance where you may be left to argue that you did not violate Title VII but may have violated the NLRA.

Many times handbook revisions should include trimming down the existing document. Handbooks sometimes become the storage place for an overabundance of policies or procedures (some of which are best kept in a separate operations manual), which could provide a roadmap for counsel to explore areas that might not arise otherwise.

**Performance Evaluations**

Performance evaluations are routine documents usually included in an employee's personnel file. This document becomes important in cases involving a termination for poor performance. In such a circumstance, the performance evaluation can either support the decision or serve to raise suspicions that an attorney can exploit.

Often times, a manager's reluctance to provide an honest and thorough evaluation results in documents stating that most employees are "meeting expectations" or "exceeding expectations" This high rating will pose a contradiction when trying to convince a jury or judge that, in reality, the employee was actually not meeting expectations. A skeptical third party will likely take these documents at face value and believe that the employee met expectations or exceeded expectations. If the manager has to explain the inconsistency by admitting that the evaluation is inaccurate, a judge or jury may surely begin to question whether the manager is being truthful.

## Disciplinary Documents

Disciplinary documents or termination sheets generally serve as a key piece of evidence detailing the employer's reasons for taking the actions that the employee claims were done for discriminatory or retaliatory motives.

If the adverse action involved a termination, the termination sheet will unquestionably be a key document. A clear explanation of the reason for the termination that is articulated at the time the event occurred can help anchor your credibility.

But when managers create these documents they may not have potential litigation in mind. This can result in vague shorthand comments such as "policy violation" or "not following directions." Where the sheet provides options for a manager to check off the reason for the termination, filling out this information in a hurry could result in selecting an inaccurate reason.

For example, the manager might select "policy violation" instead of "insubordination" where an employee has refused a direct order. Although a vague comment or an error in selecting a reason does not prove fatal to a litigation, they create scenarios where opposing counsel can exploit the error. These mistakes or oversights can be used to both question managers' credibility or embarrass them by forcing them to admit that they were careless.

## Responses to Administrative Charges

Responses to administrative charges, such as statements of position to the Equal Employment Opportunity Commission, differ from the other documents discussed since they are created after the underlying facts have taken place. These responses also usually incorporate the other common documents as exhibits or sources of information. Such responses are critical since they serve as precursors for the story that the employer will flesh out in litigation.

Since they serve as the initial opportunity for an employer to address allegations of unlawful conduct, these responses have long-lasting effects. Such documents lock the employer into certain positions. In other words, if a termination or disciplinary decision is not articulated accurately or fully in a response, clarifying or elaborating upon the reasoning at a later time may appear suspicious. Using the "blocking and tackling" metaphor here, responses to administrative charges should be concise and simple, addressing the allegations directly and accurately.

**The Bottom Line**

To sum up, the legal environment is often changing and uncertain. Nevertheless, these fundamental documents will usually appear during employment litigation, and the time and effort spent in drafting them will reduce later difficulties.

*August 2013*

*About the author and firm

Mauro Ramirez is an associate at Fisher & Phillips' Houston office. He has experience counseling clients on issues related to both federal and state employment and labor laws, including, but not limited to, Title VII of the Civil Rights Act of 1964, Age Discrimination in Employment Act, the Family Medical Leave Act, and the Fair Labor Standards Act. He also assists clients in responding to charges brought by the Equal Employment Opportunity Commission and other federal and state agencies.

For more information, contact the author at MRamirez@laborlawyers.com or (713) 292-5606. You may also visit the Fisher & Phillips' website at http://www.LaborLawyers.com.

# Chapter 26

## How to Control a Reduction in Force

by James R. Wiley*

Reductions in force (RIFs) can lead to expensive and distracting litigation, and potential liability. Unfortunately, in today's economy RIFs may be unavoidable. Nothing can make them entirely risk free, but taking certain steps can reduce the risk. The outline below identifies where the risks lay, and the guidelines describe steps designed to reduce the risk.

**Consider Alternatives to a RIF**

- RIFs bring risk. Terminated employees challenge RIFs based on myriad theories: that age, race, gender, national origin, etc. was considered in selecting employees to be RIF'd, or that the RIF disproportionately impacted any of those groups; that the RIF unlawfully precluded benefits under ERISA; that union contracts were breached; that insufficient notice of the RIF was provided to the employees; etc.
- Therefore, to avoid or minimize the liability RIFs can bring, the employer should consider alternatives. These alternatives include, for example:
    - o Furloughs and reduction in work (reduced work weeks or work days).
    - o Temporary plant shutdowns.
    - o Voluntary reverse seniority layoff with partial pay.
    - o Work-sharing.
    - o Voluntary reduced pay training programs to increase potential for interplant transfers.
    - o Use of federal job training assistance.
    - o Voluntary leaves of absence.
    - o Salary or bonus freezes; employee sharing of insurance premi-

ums, increased insurance deductible and limited benefit eligibility for newer employees.
    - Hiring freezes if attrition is high.
    - Terminating a few employees with substantial performance problems.
    - Terminating recent hires within their introductory period.
    - Discontinuing the use of temporary and part-time employees and redistributing their work.
    - Voluntary separation programs and early retirement incentives.

**Planning for a Reduction in Force**

Careful planning can minimize the risk of liability arising from a RIF. At a minimum, the employer should:

- Establish a corporate justification for the RIF.
- Create logical and consistent means and methods for the RIF.
- Establish a special management/human resources committee (including legal counsel) that will draft, implement and monitor the RIF plan. This controls the creation and flow of documentation, and selects decision makers (witnesses) in advance.
- Consider the role of diversity in the RIF. But be careful: reverse discrimination is unlawful.

**Criteria for Selecting Employees for Termination**

- Using subjective criteria is lawful, but using objective selection criteria is easier to defend to a court. It may be difficult to connect subjective criteria to the overall purpose of the RIF, or to justify them in light of performance review results.
- Centralized selection is preferred because it usually leads to more consistent procedures and results.
- Common selection methods include: seniority; historical performance evaluations; and ranking of employees.
- After employees are selected, but before they are informed, you may want to conduct an analysis to determine whether the selections will disproportionately impact a protected group. If such impact is found, you should consider using different selection criteria.

- Beware of impact on high-risk employees, such as those who are on leave or have known health issues; those whom you know are litigious; and longer-tenure employees.

**Make Sure You...**

- Document. Document all aspects of the RIF process, including the business justification for the RIF and consideration of RIF alternatives; analysis of positions to eliminate; and selection criteria.
- Train management. Train all management likely to participate in the RIF on the reason for the RIF and the procedures for implementing it, including the method and procedures for identifying jobs and ranking employees, and communicating with employees regarding the RIF.
- Protect privileged communications with counsel.
- Have a plan for exit interviews. Two members of management and/or HR should be present at every exit interview. Make sure they can deal with distraught employees. Be prepared to inform the terminating employee about: the need for the RIF and the basis of the termination decision; whether there are recall/rehire rights; severance and other benefits; and post-RIF considerations such as outplacement and re-training.
- Consider post-RIF programs. Programs for outplacement, re-training, and such build good-will, but can create liability if they are not extended equally to all employees.

**Releases and Waiver of Claims.**

Consider providing a separation/severance package or other incentive in exchange for the employee's release of all claims. Note, however, that the validity of such waivers can be problematic. For example, waivers of age discrimination claims are governed by the Older Workers Benefit Protection Act, 29 U.S.C. § 626(f), which will invalidate any waiver that does not strictly comply with very specific and sometimes convoluted requirements; and waivers of FMLA and wage (FLSA) claims may be invalid without DOL or court approval. *See* 29 CFR 825.220(d) and *Lynn's Food Store v. U.S.*, 679 F.2d 1350, 1352 (11th Cir. 1982), respectively. You should consult legal counsel if you intend to go this route.

## Providing Notice of The RIF

The federal WARN Act requires larger employers to provide notice (to affected employees and the state and local government) in advance of covered plant closings and covered mass layoffs. *See* 29 U.S.C. § 2101, *et. seq*. Notice generally must be 60 days (although there are exceptions) and rules are strict on what content the notice must include. Typically, violations require payment of wages and benefits to affected employees for the period of the violation (up to 60 days).

Whether your RIF is covered by WARN can be difficult to determine—you should consult legal counsel.

## COBRA

Do not forget the affected employees have COBRA rights. Your HR professionals will know what to do.

*July 2013*

*About the author

James R. Wiley is Co-Practice Group Leader for the Labor, Employment, and ERISA Practice Group at Carlton Fields Jorden Burt. He concentrates his practice in EEO and wage and hour law. Mr. Wiley represents management in employment litigation in federal and state courts, and before governmental agencies. He also counsels employers in risk avoidance and handles internal investigations.

# Chapter 27

## A Refresher Course for Employers on Retaliation

by Richard B. Cohen, Esq.*

"Any employment discrimination problem—sexual harassment or anything else—can always be made worse and more injurious to the conduct of the employer's business. Retaliation is guaranteed to do that. It never makes sense, it is never good for business, and it is always illegal." This is from an Equal Employment Opportunity Commission ("EEOC") lawyer. And retaliation comprises almost 40% (and rising) of all EEOC charges, the most frequently filed charge with the EEOC.

Two new government announcements will preface and underscore the need for this tutorial.

A New Retaliation Lawsuit and Settlement

Recently, the EEOC announced that it has sued an Alabama company contending that it retaliated against one of its managers for firing an employee who had sexually harassed and assaulted a female co-worker. The suit alleges that the employer verbally abused him, re-hired the harasser, and terminated the manager when he declared that he would "tell the truth" about the matter.

And the Justice Department just settled a case against a city in which it was alleged that the city discriminated against an employee by subjecting her to sexual harassment (unwanted sexual advances by a co-worker) and then firing her when she complained and filed an EEOC charge. The complaint alleges that the city fired her for making internal complaints and filing a sex discrimination charge with the EEOC.

The cases keep coming and the filing of retaliation charges will continue at an alarming rate.

What Is Retaliation?

Retaliation is far easier to prove (and difficult to defend against) than the underlying discrimination, and even if the underlying claim of discrimination has no merit, retaliation can *still* be claimed and proved. All that must be shown to make out a claim for retaliation is: (1) that plaintiff was engaged in a "statutorily protected activity" by opposing an employment practice that she has a good faith, reasonable basis to believe is unlawful; (2) an "adverse employment action" by the employer; and (3) some causal connection between the two.

An employee who alleges or files a discrimination claim or complaint is protected from retaliation—in our parlance, the employee becomes insulated or "cocooned"—because it is extremely difficult or even next to impossible to take *any* adverse employment action at that point for fear of incurring a retaliation charge.

Pretty much anything you can do can be claimed to be an "adverse act" against an employee who has filed a complaint of discrimination, and therefore retaliatory (and employees have, indeed, claimed just about everything). Termination, of course, is an adverse act, but adverse acts can also be demotion, transfer, ignoring or berating an employee, taking away work or responsibility, or giving too much work, and even refusing to re-hire.

A claim of sexual harassment by a supervisor is particularly susceptible to a follow-up retaliation claim since virtually any adverse action against the employee can be viewed as retaliation.

Preventing Retaliation Claims

To prevent retaliation claims, you first must take all steps to prevent any discrimination claims. You know the drill—zero tolerance policies, up-to-date employee manuals, training (and more training) for all managers and employees, and open communications with employees especially about reporting discrimination.

As to what to do after an employee has filed a charge or claim of discrimination, an employer's best practice is to take a "business as usual" approach and act as if no complaint had been filed by treating the employee like any other employee; engaging in open, non-intimidating communication with the employee to find common ground while the investigation or litigation is pending; and, of course, documenting all decisions and pre and post-complaint performance issues that might result in discipline.

*April 2013*

*About the author and firm

Richard B. Cohen, Esq. is a member of the national law firm Fox Rothschild LLP, and based in its New York City office. He is a litigator and employment lawyer. Mr. Cohen lectures and writes often on employment and trial law, and is editor/writer of the firm's popular blog "*Employment Discrimination Report*," from which this article is adapted. His firm bio is at: http://www.foxrothschild.com/attorneys/richard-cohen.html, and he can be reached at (212) 878-7900.

Disclaimer: This article does not, and is not intended to, constitute legal advice, nor is it intended as a source of advertising or solicitation. You should not rely on the information provided in this article without first obtaining separate legal advice, and you should always seek the advice of competent legal counsel in your own state.

# Chapter 28

## Three Questions Employers Should Ask About Religious Accommodation Requests

by Daniel H. Handman, Esq.*

A recent survey by the Pew Research Center reports that 58% of Americans say that religion is very important in their lives and 76% of Americans say that prayer is an important part of their daily lives. The survey also shows that an increasing number of Americans adhere to religions, like Islam, Hinduism, Buddhism and Mormonism, which were not nearly as prevalent 20 years ago. To be sure, the increase in diversity of religions and the large number of Americans that closely observe religious practices has led to increased challenges for American employers, especially when those practices conflict with workplace requirements. Those challenges have been laid bare by a recent decision from a federal judge in San Francisco finding that Abercrombie & Fitch had discriminated against a Muslim employee by refusing to allow her to wear a hijab, a head scarf, while at work.

Abercrombie has a "Look Policy" which requires employees to wear clothes similar to those sold in stores and it prohibits employees from wearing any type of headwear. After several months, a regional manager came for a regularly scheduled visit at a Northern California store and he saw that Umme-Hani Khan, a saleswoman, was wearing a hijab. The manager twice asked Khan to remove her hijab and she said she could not because it was a part of her religion. Ultimately, Abercrombie terminated Khan's employment.

In *EEOC v. Abercrombie & Fitch Stores, Inc.*, Judge Yvonne Gonzalez Rogers of the Northern District of California took the rare step of granting summary judgment to the EEOC, finding that Abercrombie discriminated against Khan because of her religion by terminating her employment for refusing to take off her hijab at work. In particular, Judge

Rogers found that Khan's request to wear a hijab was a sincerely held religious belief, that it conflicted with the "Look Policy" and that wearing a hijab did not pose an "undue hardship" on Abercrombie. In particular, Judge Rogers found that the company's belief that Khan's dress would affect store performance or brand image was an "unsubstantiated opinion" that was not supported by hard evidence.

The decision has been controversial, not only because it involves a prominent retailer with stores in malls and shopping centers all across the country. It also exposes an increasing conflict between employers, especially in retail and service industries, who find that their employees' religious practices have a tangible detriment on their business.

For practical purposes, the *Abercrombie* decision highlights three common issues faced by employers involving an employee's religious practices.

### 1. Does An Employee's Bona Fide Religious Belief Conflict with an Employment Duty?

In the *Abercrombie* case, there was no question that the "Look Policy" conflicted with Khan's religious belief, since it expressly prohibited an employee from wearing any type of headwear, including a hijab. But, it is not always that clear. Consider *Chenzira v. Cincinnati Children's Hospital*, a recent decision involving a hospital in Cincinnati that required its medical professionals to get flu vaccines. An employee refused to do so because the flu vaccines all contain animal byproducts and she was a vegan. The EEOC sued and a judge refused to dismiss the claim on the ground that veganism is not a religion, but rather a dietary restriction or an ethical belief.

Would that decision stand up on appellate review? Probably not. An appellate court has already rejected the notion that veganism is a religion, both because there is nothing religious about refusing to eat animal byproducts and also because one can only imagine the floodgates that such a decision would open if it were upheld.

But it does expose significant issues that employers must consider. One important issue is whether an employee has a bona fide religious belief.

In *Chenzira*, despite what the judge said, veganism is almost certainly not a religion. But in the *Abercrombie* case, there is no question that Islam is a religion and there was no question that the employee was a practicing Muslim.

An employee need not be devout in order to avail himself of his right to legal protection. But, at the same time, the religious matter for which he needs an accommodation must actually be: (1) an obligation, not a preference; and (2) an obligation sincerely adhered to.

In the *Abercrombie* case, for example, Islam arguably requires women to wear a head covering, but not all Muslim women do it. Had this employee not regularly worn a hijab, then the result would have unquestionably been different.

### 2. Does an Accommodation Impose an Undue Hardship?

Even when an employee has a sincerely held religious belief that conflicts with his work, an employer does not have to accommodate it when doing so would impose an "undue hardship" on the employer. But what is and is not an undue hardship varies from case to case, depending on the nature of the accommodation requested, the size of the employer and the nature of the hardship that is imposed.

Although there are many cases which stand for the proposition that anything more than a *de minimis* cost on an employer causes an undue hardship, the means of proving a hardship have proven elusive. The *Abercrombie* case exemplifies this dilemma perfectly. Numerous employees testified that deviation from its Look Policy would "detract from the in store experience and negative affect its brand." But the court found that testimony to be self-serving and speculative. There was no objective proof that economic harm or any harm would befall the store by allowing employees to wear religious dress.

Compare that to a line of cases involving public safety positions where the courts have found that an employer's need to ban the wearing of yarmulkes or dreadlocks by fire and police officers was legitimate. In those cases, the courts have found that the public safety interest involved heavily outweighs the need for a religious accommodation.

So, how do employers gauge whether an undue hardship exists? There are a few hard and fast rules. Generally speaking, a requested accommodation imposes an undue hardship if: (1) it would require an employer to take action that would harm other employees; (2) it would put the employee or the employer's customers in risk of harm; (3) it would violate a collective bargaining agreement; or (4) it would impose some tangible, measurable harm. In the *Abercrombie* case, the judge found that none of these hallmarks was present or, at least, there was not enough evidence that the store would suffer tangible harm.

### 3. Are *Any* Reasonable Accommodations Available?

The requirement to provide a reasonable accommodation to employees is tied in large part to the undue hardship issue. The courts employ a "no harm, no foul" methodology. That is, if an employer can establish that the only accommodation to an employee would impose an undue burden on it, then it has no obligation to try to find a reasonable accommodation for the employee. And an employer does not need to provide an employee with the specific accommodation he requested; it only has to provide a reasonable accommodation.

In most cases, employers would be well-served to do what they do when an employee asks for an accommodation to a disability. That is, when an employee requests an accommodation to a religious practice, the employer should have an interactive discussion with the employee—a brainstorming session—to see if there is some way that the employee's religious obligations can be accommodated without imposing a burden on the employer's operations.

For example, in *Daniels v. City of Arlington*, a city did exactly the right thing when it refused a police officer's request to wear a religious symbol on his uniform. But rather than issuing an ultimatum, the city sat down with the officer and offered him three alternatives, namely to wear the symbol on a bracelet, on a necklace under his uniform, or to transfer to a non-uniformed job. The court dismissed the case because the employee rejected all three proposals.

* * * *

To be sure, not all cases will allow for clean endings to seemingly intractable disputes. But the more effort an employer puts in to find a reasonable accommodation, the more likely a court will be to grant judgment to the employer.

Religious accommodation cases are unquestionably on the rise with the increase in diversity of religions and the number of Americans who view religion as very important in their lives. Not every religious accommodation case is cut and dry and most involve several simultaneously moving parts.

But unlike many issues, there is a body of law on religious accommodations and it is relatively straightforward. By asking and answering the three questions in this article, employers should be able to navigate this minefield successfully.

*October 2013*

*About the author and firm

Dan Handman is a partner in the Los Angeles office of Hirschfeld Kraemer, a California labor and employment law boutique. Mr. Handman represents employers exclusively in matters involving claims of discrimination, harassment, wage-hour violations and trade secret claims. He is also an expert in traditional labor law and has represented employers around the country on matters involving labor unions. He is the editor of the California Workplace Advisor, a labor and employment law blog (http://blog.hkemploymentlaw.com). You can reach Mr. Handman by e-mail at dhandman@hkemploymentlaw.com.

# Chapter 29

# Seven Employment Topics to Consider When Hiring Seasonal Workers

by Steven F. Pockrass*

As 2013 comes to an end, we consider several employment issues about which employers must be aware if they plan to hire seasonal workers. This year, Black Friday started on Thursday in many stores, and Cyber Monday turned into a three-day cyber weekend. In preparation for the holiday season, many retailers beefed up their employment ranks by hiring a cadre of short-term workers. To make this a merry experience, businesses should plan carefully and not cut corners when hiring and onboarding for the holidays.

## Employment Eligibility and anti-Discrimination Laws

Employers should remember that applicants for seasonal positions are subject to the same employment eligibility verification requirements as non-seasonal workers. In addition, seasonal workers receive the same protections against discrimination, harassment, and retaliation as non-seasonal workers under most federal, state, and local anti-discrimination laws. Seasonal workers also can create the same potential liabilities for their employers as their non-seasonal peers if they engage in discrimination, harassment, or other inappropriate conduct.

## Wage & Hour Issues

Just as with non-seasonal employees, setting proper expectations and effectively documenting communications with seasonal workers is a must. Most seasonal jobs are not exempt from overtime under the federal Fair Labor Standards Act (FLSA) or state wage and hour laws. Lawsuits brought under federal and state law are extremely popular right now among plaintiffs' lawyers, particularly those alleging that employees were pressured to work through lunch breaks or before or after their shifts without being paid for that time.

Given these trends, employers need to have strong policies and procedures with respect to clocking in and clocking out and with respect to prohibiting off-the-clock work. Notably, many retailers remain open for extended hours during the holidays, so employers should clearly communicate their expectations regarding work schedules—and not just the number of hours to be worked—to all employees. Employers also need to plan work schedules well in order to avoid incurring unanticipated overtime costs.

## Students & Minors

Many people who apply for seasonal employment are students. Particularly if this is a first job, these individuals may not understand the gravity of properly clocking in and clocking out, or they may be willing to work extra hours in order to make a good impression. So emphasizing wage and hour compliance with students and their supervisors is especially important.

Employers also must ensure that they are complying with all applicable federal and state child labor laws. These include laws requiring students to have work permits, laws that place limits on the number of hours or how late in the evening minors may work, and laws that mandate breaks for younger workers.

## At-Will Employment

Employers want to be sure that they are telling all seasonal hires in writing when their seasonal employment is expected to end. Most seasonal employment is intended to be at will, and employers also must be sure to communicate that to seasonal hires clearly and in writing. It is always wise to consult with legal counsel regarding the terminology that should be used in offer letters or other communications to new hires to avoid giving the impression that at-will employees, whether seasonal or non-seasonal, are "permanent" or are employed for a "definite term."

## Minimum Wage Laws

In many states, new employment laws and increases in the minimum wage become effective on January 1. While employers should be planning now for those changes regardless of whether they have seasonal employees, they also need to think about how those laws will impact seasonal workers who stay on past December 31.

## Record-keeping Requirements

Employers need to be sure that they have the people and the record-keeping systems in place to handle a sudden influx of new employees. Maintaining accurate records is important not only with respect to immediate issues such as payroll, but also down the road. Below are some examples.

- Seasonal employment counts toward the 12-month portion of the eligibility requirements for coverage under the federal Family and Medical Leave Act (FMLA). So employers' record-keeping systems must be able to track and aggregate non-continuous periods of employment.
- Seasonal employees may become witnesses in future lawsuits, so it is valuable to have accurate records of when and where they were on duty and of how to reach them after their seasonal employment ends.
- Seasonal employment sometimes continues beyond the holidays and can turn into a non-seasonal relationship. Employers want to be sure that any such change in status does not slip through the cracks. Thus, employers should have a quality system in place that properly codes and updates any information that affects anniversary dates, review dates, step pay increases, etc.

## Onboarding

The onboarding process for seasonal employees is just as important, and arguably more important, than the onboarding process for year-round employees. Consider the examples that follow.

- The holiday season is a busy time, which means managers have fewer opportunities to provide on-the-job training to seasonal workers and to integrate them into the company's culture.

- Holiday shoppers tend to be stressed and impatient. So seasonal employees need to be able to hit the ground running and provide quality customer service from the start of their employment, even if they lack prior experience working for a particular employer.

- The same rules of conduct apply to seasonal workers as to non-seasonal workers, so seasonal workers need to be trained immediately as to what these rules are.

- Non-seasonal workers also should be trained regarding the appropriate treatment of seasonal workers.

- Some employers choose to apply a more rigid standard of attendance to seasonal workers than they apply to non-seasonal workers. Employers might do this because of the intended short-term nature of the relationship and the added importance of having people at work and on time for the holiday retail rush. Employers that adopt a more rigid seasonal attendance policy should emphasize the policy during the onboarding process and communicate it in writing to seasonal hires.

- Some workers return to the same employer every holiday season and, because of their prior experience, may think that they already know all of the employer's policies and procedures. So if any policies or procedures have changed since the last holiday season, it will be important to make these repeat seasonal workers aware of the changes.

- Significant discounts that retailers offer during seasonal sales can result in large crowds that have caused trampling injuries to both workers and customers. In anticipation of this problem, the U.S. Department of Labor (DOL) recently issued a press release on crowd management issues including a link to the fact sheet issued by the Occupational Safety and Health Administration on crowd safety guidelines for retailers. As an initial matter, all employers should develop and implement a crowd management plan. In addition, employers should train both seasonal hires and year-round employees who will be working during holiday sales on this plan.

*November 2013*

*About the author and firm

Steven F. Pockrass is a shareholder in the Indianapolis office of Ogletree, Deakins, Nash, Smoak & Stewart, P.C. (Ogletree Deakins), where he Chairs the firm's Wage and Hour Practice Group. Ogletree Deakins is a law firm with over 700 lawyers in 45 cities in the United States and in Europe. The firm represents employers exclusively in all aspects of labor and employment law. For additional information about Ogletree Deakins visit its website at http://blog.hkemploymentlaw.com.

*This article was writtenby Ogletree Deakins, a labor and employment law firm that represents management. This information should not be relied upon as legal advice.*

# Chapter 30

## Avoiding Pitfalls of Severance Agreements

by Rachelle E. Hill*

As a business owner, it is inevitable that there will come a time when, for some reason or another, you will need to terminate an employee. In many circumstances an employer will use a severance agreement to obtain a release for any potential liability under which a severance amount will be paid. As with many employee-employer issues, there are certain potential pitfalls that surround severance agreements that an employer needs to take into consideration when offering severance.

**Put the Agreement in Writing:** This first issue seems like an obvious requirement, but in the event an employer is offering severance payment it is a best business practice to put it in a writing that contains a release for the employer. Unless agreed to otherwise, an employer is under no obligation to offer severance pay. In the event the employer wants to pay such amounts, it needs to get the agreement memorialized in writing.

**Avoid Waiver of Future Claims:** An employee cannot effectively waive a future claim under a severance agreement. Therefore, if the agreement is provided when the employee is still employed, it is important the employee signs the agreement on the last day of the employment. Otherwise an employee could sign the agreement and release all claims and then a claim could arise following the release. The release is only effective for claims existing at the time the agreement is signed and will not prevent a lawsuit for a future act.

**Avoid Overly Broad Language:** While employers hope to obtain a broad release of any future legal action, there are certain rights an employee cannot waive, such as the right to file a charge of discrimination with the EEOC or to testify in any hearing conducted by the EEOC. Employers must be careful to not include overly broad releases in their severance agreements that may be construed as impairing an employee's right to file an EEOC charge post-separation.

Recently, the EEOC has become more proactive and has initiated suits to combat what it believes are overly broad release and non-disparagement language that may lead the employee to think he or she could not file an administrative action. In *EEOC v. Baker & Taylor*, the EEOC filed suit in the United States District Court of Illinois claiming that the release violated federal law by "conditioning the receipt of severance benefits on employees' agreement to a severance agreement that deterred the filing of charges and interfered with their ability to communicate voluntarily with the EEOC. . ." The case was resolved by a consent decree entered on July 10, 2013, under which Baker and Taylor agreed to revise its agreements to remove language barring the initiation of a suit with an administrative agency of the United States and from discussing or commenting on the company in a manner that would "reflect negatively on the company." In addition, Baker & Taylor agreed to use the following language in all severance agreements that sought a release:

> Nothing in this Agreement is intended to limit in any way an Employee's right or ability to file a charge or claim of discrimination with the U.S. Equal Employment Opportunity Commission ("EEOC") or comparable state or local agencies. These agencies have the authority to carry out their statutory duties by investigating the charge, issuing a determination, filing a lawsuit in Federal or state court in their own name, or taking any other action authorized under these statutes. Employees retain the right to participate in such any [sic] action and to recover any appropriate relief. Employees retain the right to communicate with the EEOC and comparable state or local agencies and such communication can be initiated by the employee or in response to the government and is not limited by any non-disparagement obligation under this agreement.

**Comply with the Older Workers Benefit Protection Act (OWBA):** Employers with 20 or more employees need to be aware of the OWBA when terminating an employee who is 40 years and older. The OWBA is a section within the Age Discrimination in Employment Act (ADEA) that establishes strict requirements for an employer to "knowingly and voluntarily" release ADEA claims. Among other requirements, to be considered a valid ADEA waiver, a severance agreement must at a minimum include the following:

- be in writing and be understandable;
- specifically refer to ADEA rights or claims;
- not waive rights or claims that may arise in the future;
- be in exchange for valuable consideration in addition to that which the employee is already entitled; and
- advise the individual in writing to consult an attorney before signing the waiver.

**Additionally, it is imperative that an employer provide the employee at least 21 days to review the agreement and an additional 7 days to revoke the agreement after signing it.**

**Termination of Multiple Employees:** There are additional requirements when an employer is terminating the employee as part of a group. This applies in both voluntary situations, such as an exit incentive program where an employee is provided additional consideration to voluntarily resign and sign a waiver, and in an involuntary termination. Specifically an employer must provide at least 45 days for an employee to consider the waiver and give written notice of information on the "decisional unit"—the group under which the employer selected the layoffs—that identifies the employees to be terminated and those who were not, along with job titles and ages. This requirement is directed at illustrating any potential disparate effect a layoff may have on an older employee in order for the employee to "knowingly" release a potential claim.

**Conclusion:** This article does not cover all issues that can occur in severance agreements and is only meant to highlight certain pitfalls. We encourage all business owners to utilize legal counsel when negotiating severance agreements. At a minimum, a company should have its standard severance agreement form reviewed to ensure there are no major issues with the boilerplate language and its own customary policy for offering and negotiating severance amounts. Employers are under no obligation to provide severance pay; therefore, it is important to ensure that in reality the agreement does what the employer believes it does instead of paying significant sums to find the agreement is unenforceable.

*January 2014*

*About the author

Rachelle E. Hill is an attorney at Bean, Kinney & Korman, P.C. in Arlington, Virginia. She practices in the areas of employment law and commercial litigation. For more information, she can be contacted at rhill@beankinney.com or 703.525.4000.

# Chapter 31

## Title VII Does Not Cover Sexual Orientation... Or Does It?

by T. Harold Pinkley*

From the time I began practicing employment law many (too many) years ago, and probably for longer than that, we employment types have been quite comfortable in advising our clients that Title VII does not cover sexual orientation; in other words, when it comes to the homosexual or bisexual employee, discriminate away. It has become fairly clear, however, that that rather glib advice is incomplete and perhaps even wrong.

In a recent case against a federal agency, the EEOC ruled that a claim of "gender identity, change of sex, and/or transgender status" is covered by Title VII. *Macy v. Bureau of Alcohol, Tobacco, Firearms and Explosives*, EEOC Appeal No. 0120120821 (Apr. 20, 2012). After being offered a job conditioned upon a background check, Ms. Macy notified the BATFE that she was transitioning from male to female. Less than a week later, she was notified that the position had been filled by someone else.

Ms. Macy then filed a complaint with the agency alleging that she had been discriminated against on the basis of sex, adding that she was also alleging gender identity and sex stereotyping by the agency. The EEOC held on appeal that Title VII's prohibition of discrimination based on sex included not only "biological sex, but also gender stereotyping—failing to act and appear according to expectations defined by gender." The EEOC based this conclusion on its reading of several cases, most importantly the Supreme Court's decision in *Price Waterhouse v. Hopkins*, 490 U.S. 228 (1989) and some of its progeny. In *Price Waterhouse*, the Court found that Title VII's provisions were violated when an employer discriminated against an individual for failing to conform to "gender-based expectations." The EEOC's decision, however, went further than

*Price Waterhouse* in finding that gender stereotyping, which is relied on by most of the courts that have found that Title VII protects transgender employees, is not the only way to prove sex discrimination. The EEOC went on to find that valid theories of sex discrimination include actions motivated by "hostility, a desire to protect people of a certain gender, by assumptions that disadvantage men, by gender stereotypes, or by the desire to accommodate other people's prejudices or discomfort . . . ."

Neither the EEOC nor the courts have taken the next step and found that discrimination based on sexual orientation is a form of sex stereotyping, but it takes no great leap of imagination to see the argument. Being born male and presenting female is certainly no more a failure to live up to sexual stereotypes than being sexually attracted to others of one's own sex. It is difficult to see any meaningful difference for these purposes between being homosexual and being transgender, and it is quite reasonable to expect that before long either a court or the EEOC will agree.

In light of this possibility—which I would characterize more as a probability—the prudent employer will take steps now to avoid liability in the future, including:

- Revising HR policies to include a prohibition of sex discrimination, specifically including a prohibition of sex stereotyping;
- Modifying, if necessary, pre-employment background checks;
- Reviewing and making necessary changes to the restroom and changing or locker room policies, dress codes, issuance of new employee identification documents, and the like;
- Investigating the possibility of including coverage under the company's health insurance for transition-related medical procedures; and
- Perhaps most importantly, including sex stereotyping in your anti-discrimination training at all levels of the company.

[Addendum: Since this article was written, a couple of notable developments have occurred: First, EEOC Commissioner Chai Feldblum wrote an op-ed piece in The New York Times, published on March 24, 2014, stating her position that sexual orientation discrimination is forbidden by Title VII. http://www.nytimes.com/roomfordebate/2014/03/24/if-gays-can-marry-and-be-fired-for-doing-so/existing-law-often-applies-to-discrimination-against-gays (last visited on April 17, 2014); second, in *Ter-Veer v. Billington*, U.S.D.C., D.D.C., March 31, 2014, Civil No. 12-1290, a federal district judge in Washington, D.C., decided that the plaintiff's claim that he had been discriminated against because of his sexual orientation could go forward.]

*September 2013*

*<u>About the author and firm</u>

This article is a general reflection on a current legal issue. It is not intended to be legal advice and should not be taken as such.

Harold Pinkley is a partner in the Labor & Employment Practice Group of Butler Snow LLP. He practices in the firm's Nashville, Tennessee, office handling a broad range of employment litigation, from single-plaintiff discrimination and retaliation cases to large class actions all across the country. If you have any questions regarding discrimination or harassment in your workplace, please contact the author or any of Butler Snow's Labor and Employment attorneys for guidance.

Butler Snow is a full-service law firm with more than 280 attorneys representing local, regional, national and international clients from 17 offices globally. Ranked as one of America's Top 100 law firms in the BTI Power Rankings, Butler Snow is recognized as one of the nation's top law firms for client service. The firm was recently ranked 48th out of 650 firms in the BTI Client Relationship Scorecard for understanding our client's business, anticipating client's needs, unprompted communication, legal skills, quality and keeping clients informed. For more information, visit http://www.butlersnow.com or follow Butler Snow on twitter @Butler_Snow.

# Chapter 32
# Ownership of Business-Related Social Media Accounts

by Aaron Rubin and Anelia V. Delcheva*

Social media platforms have become an increasingly important means for companies to build and manage their brands and to interact with their customers, in many cases eclipsing companies' traditional ".com" websites. Social media providers typically make their platforms available to users without charge, but companies nevertheless invest significant time and other resources to create and maintain their presences on those providers' platforms. A company's social media page or profile and its associated followers, friends and other connections are often considered to be valuable business assets.

But who owns these valuable assets—the company or the individual employee who manages the company's page or profile? Social media's inherently interactive nature has created an important role for these individual employees. Such an employee essentially acts as the "voice" of the company and his or her style and personality may be essential to the success and popularity of that company's social media presence. As a result, the lines between "company brand" and "personal brand" may become blurred over time. And when the company and the individual part ways, that blurring can raise difficult issues, both legal and logistical, regarding the ownership and valuation of business-related social media accounts.

Such issues have arisen in a number of cases recently, several of which we discuss below. Although these cases leave open a number of questions, the message to companies who use social media is loud and clear: it is imperative to proactively establish policies and practices that address ownership and use of business-related social media accounts.

### *PhoneDog v. Kravitz*

A recently settled California case, *PhoneDog v. Kravitz*, Case No. C 11-03474 (N.D. Cal.), raised a number of interesting issues around the ownership and valuation of social media accounts. The defendant, Noah Kravitz, worked for the plaintiff, PhoneDog, a mobile news and reviews website. While he was employed by PhoneDog, Kravitz used the Twitter handle "@PhoneDog_Noah" to provide product reviews, eventually accumulating 17,000 Twitter followers over a period of approximately four and a half years. Kravitz then left PhoneDog to work for one of its competitors but he maintained control of the Twitter account and changed the account handle to "@noahkravitz." When Kravitz refused PhoneDog's request to relinquish the Twitter account that had been previously associated with the "@PhoneDog_Noah" handle, PhoneDog filed a complaint against Kravitz asserting various claims, including trade secret misappropriation, conversion, and intentional and negligent interference with economic advantage.

Kravitz filed a motion to dismiss the complaint based on a number of arguments, including PhoneDog's inability to establish that it had suffered damages in excess of the $75,000 jurisdictional threshold. Kravitz also disputed PhoneDog's ownership interest in either the Twitter account or its followers, based on Twitter's terms of service, which state that Twitter accounts belong to Twitter and not to Twitter users such as PhoneDog. Finally, Kravitz argued that Twitter followers are "human beings who have the discretion to subscribe and/or unsubscribe" to the account and are not PhoneDog's property, and asserted that "[t]o date, the industry precedent has been that absent an agreement prohibiting any employee from doing so, after an employee leaves an employer, they are free to change their Twitter handle."

With respect to the amount-in-controversy issue, PhoneDog asserted that Kravitz's continued use of the "@noahkravitz" handle resulted in at least $340,000 in damages, an amount that was calculated based on the total number of followers, the time during which Kravitz had control over the account, and a purported "industry standard" value of $2.50 per Twitter follower. Kravitz argued that any value attributed to the Twitter account came from his efforts in posting tweets and the followers' interest in him, not from the account itself. Kravitz also disputed PhoneDog's purported industry standard value of $2.50 per Twitter follower, and contended that valuation of the account required consideration of a number of factors, including (1) the number of followers, (2) the number of tweets, (3) the content of the tweets, (4) the person publishing the tweets, and (5) the person placing the value on the account.

With respect to the ownership issue, PhoneDog claimed that it had an ownership interest in the account based on the license to use and access the account granted to it in the Twitter terms of service, and also that it had an ownership interest in the content posted on the account. PhoneDog also pointed to a purported "intangible property interest" in the Twitter account's list of followers, which PhoneDog compared to a business customer list. Finally, PhoneDog asserted that, regardless of any ownership interest in the account, PhoneDog was entitled to damages based on Kravitz's interference with PhoneDog's access to and use of the account, which (among other things) purportedly affected PhoneDog's economic relations with its advertisers.

The court determined that the amount-in-controversy issue was intertwined with factual and legal issues raised by PhoneDog's claims and, therefore, could not be resolved at the motion-to-dismiss stage. Accordingly, the court denied without prejudice Kravitz's motion to dismiss for lack of subject matter jurisdiction. The court also denied Kravitz's motion to dismiss PhoneDog's trade secret and conversion claims, but granted Kravitz's motion to dismiss PhoneDog's claims of interference with prospective economic advantage.

The parties subsequently settled the dispute, so, unfortunately, we will never know how the court would have ruled on the variety of interesting issues that the case presented. Interestingly, although the terms of the settlement remain confidential, as of mid-September, Kravitz appears to have kept control of the Twitter account and its attendant followers. It is worth noting that the case might have been more straightforward—and the result more favorable to the company—had PhoneDog established clear policies regarding the ownership of business-related social media accounts.

***Ardis Health, LLC et al. v. Nankivell***

A New York case, *Ardis Health, LLC et al. v. Nankivell*, Case No. 11 Civ. 5013 (S.D.N.Y.), more clearly illustrates the fundamental point that companies should proactively establish policies and practices that address the ownership and use of business-related social media accounts.

The plaintiffs in *Ardis Health* were a group of closely affiliated online marketing companies that develop and market herbal and beauty products. The defendant was a former employee who had held a position at Ardis Health, LLC as a "Video and Social Media Producer." Following her termination, the defendant refused to turn over to the plaintiffs the login information and passwords for the social media accounts that she had managed for the plaintiffs during her employment. The plaintiffs then filed a lawsuit against the defendant and sought a preliminary injunction seeking, among other things, to compel her to provide them with that access information.

Fortunately for the plaintiffs, they had required the defendant to execute an agreement at the commencement of her employment that stated in part that all work created or developed by defendant "shall be the sole and exclusive property" of one of the plaintiffs, and that required the defendant to return all confidential information to the company upon request. This employment agreement also stipulated that "actual or threatened breach . . . will cause [the plaintiff] irreparable injury and damage." On these facts, the court noted that "[i]t is uncontested that plaintiffs own the rights to" the social media account access information that the defendant had refused to provide. Interestingly, the court held that the plaintiffs were likely to prevail on their conversion claim, effectively treating the disputed social media account access information as a form of intangible personal property. The court also determined that plaintiffs were suffering irreparable harm as a result of the defendant's refusal to turn over that access information. Accordingly, the court granted the plaintiffs' motion for a preliminary injunction ordering the defendant to turn over the disputed login information and passwords to the plaintiffs.

As far as we can tell from the reported decision in *Ardis Health*, the defendant's employment agreement did not expressly address the ownership or use of social media accounts or any related access information.

Nonetheless, even the fairly generic work product ownership and confidentiality language included in the defendant's employment agreement, as noted above, appears to have been an important factor in the favorable outcome for the plaintiffs, which illustrates the advantages of addressing these issues contractually with employees—in advance, naturally. And as discussed below, companies can put themselves in an even stronger position by incorporating more explicit terms concerning social media into their employment agreements.

### *Eagle v. Morgan and Maremont v. Fredman*

Former employers aren't always the plaintiffs in cases regarding the ownership of business-related social media accounts. In an interesting twist, two other cases—*Eagle v. Morgan*, Case No. 11-4303 (E.D. Pa.), and *Maremont v. Fredman*, Case No. 10 C 7811 (N.D. Ill.)—were brought by employees who alleged that their employers had taken over and started using social media accounts that the employees considered to be personal accounts.

*Eagle* began as a dispute over an ex-employee's LinkedIn account and her related LinkedIn connections. The plaintiff, Dr. Linda Eagle, was a founder of the defendant company, Edcomm. Dr. Eagle alleged that, following her termination, Edcomm personnel changed her LinkedIn password and account profile, including by replacing her name and photograph with the name and photo of the company's new CEO. Among the various claims filed by each party, in pretrial rulings, the court granted Dr. Eagle's motion to dismiss Edcomm's trade secret claim and granted Edcomm's motion for summary judgment on Dr. Eagle's Computer Fraud and Abuse Act (CFAA) and Lanham Act claims.

Regarding the trade secret claim, the court held that LinkedIn connections did not constitute trade secrets because they were "either generally known in the wider business community or capable of being easily derived from public information." Regarding her CFAA claims, the court concluded that the damages Dr. Eagle claimed she had suffered—putatively arising from harm to reputation, goodwill and business opportunities—were insufficient to satisfy the "loss" element of a CFAA claim, which requires some relation to "the impairment or damage to a computer or computer system." Finally, in rejecting the plaintiff's claim that

Edcomm violated the Lanham Act by posting the new CEO's name and picture on the LinkedIn account previously associated with Dr. Eagle, the court found that Dr. Eagle could not demonstrate that Edcomm's actions caused a "likelihood of confusion," as required by the Act.

Eventually, the *Eagle* case proceeded to trial. The court ultimately held for Dr. Eagle on her claim of unauthorized use of name under the Pennsylvania statute that protects a person's commercial interest in his or her name or likeness, her claim of invasion of privacy by misappropriation of identity, and her claim of misappropriation of publicity. The court also rejected Edcomm's counterclaims for misappropriation and unfair competition. Meanwhile, the court held for the defendants on Dr. Eagle's claims of identity theft, conversion, tortious interference with contract, civil conspiracy, and civil aiding and abetting. Although the court's decision reveals that Edcomm did have certain policies in place regarding establishment and use of business-related social media accounts by employees, unfortunately for Edcomm, those policies do not appear to have clearly addressed ownership of those accounts or the disposition of those accounts after employees leave the company.

In any event, although Dr. Eagle did prevail on a number of her claims, the court concluded that she was unable to establish that she had suffered any damages. Dr. Eagle put forth a creative damages formula that attributed her total past revenue to business generated by her LinkedIn contacts in order to establish a per contact value, and then used that value to calculate her damages for the period of time when she was unable to access her account. But the court held that Dr. Eagle's damages request was insufficient for a number of reasons, primarily that she was unable to establish the fact of damages with reasonable certainty. The court also denied Dr. Eagle's request for punitive damages. Therefore, despite prevailing on a number of her claims, Dr. Eagle's victory in the case was somewhat pyrrhic.

In *Maremont*, the plaintiff, Jill Maremont, was seriously injured in a car accident and had to spend several months rehabilitating away from work. While recovering, Ms. Maremont's employer, Susan Fredman Design Group, posted and tweeted promotional messages on Ms. Maremont's personal Facebook and Twitter accounts, where she had developed a large following as a well-known interior designer. Although Ms. Maremont asked her employer to stop posting and tweeting, the defendant continued to do so. Ms. Maremont then brought claims against Susan Fredman Design Group under the Lanham Act, the Illinois Right of Publicity Act, and the Stored Communications Act, as well as a common law right to privacy claim. The parties filed cross-motions for summary judgment, which the court denied with respect to the Lanham Act and Stored Communications Act claims, largely due to lack of evidence on whether or not Ms. Maremont suffered actual damages as a result of her employer's actions. The court granted Susan Fredman Design Group's motion for summary judgment with respect to Ms. Maremont's right of publicity claim, based on the fact that the defendant did not actually impersonate Ms. Maremont when it used her accounts. The court also granted Susan Fredman Design Group's motion for summary judgment with respect to Ms. Maremont's right of privacy claim because the "matters discussed in Maremont's Facebook and Twitter posts were not private and that Maremont did not try to keep any such facts private."

***Proactive Steps***

Considering how vital social media accounts are to today's companies, and given the lack of clear applicable law concerning the ownership of such accounts, companies should take proactive steps to protect these valuable business assets.

For example, companies should consider clearly addressing the ownership of company social media accounts in agreements with their employees, such as employee proprietary information and invention assignment agreements. Agreements like this should state, in part, that all social media accounts that employees register or manage as part of their job duties or using company resources—including all associated account names and handles, pages, profiles, followers and content—are the property of the company, and that all login information and passwords for such accounts are both the property and the confidential information of the company and must be returned to the company upon termination or at any other time upon the company's request. In general, companies should not permit employees to post under their own names on company social media accounts or use their own names as account names or handles. If particular circumstances require an employee or other individual to post under his or her own name—for example, where the company has engaged a well-known industry expert or commentator to manage the account—the company might want to go a step further and include even more specific contractual provisions that address ownership rights to the account at issue.

In parallel, companies should implement and enforce social media policies that provide employees with clear guidance regarding the appropriate use of business-related social media accounts, including instructions on how to avoid blurring the lines between company and personal accounts. (Keep in mind, however, that social media policies need to be carefully drafted so as not to run afoul of the National Labor Relations Act, state laws restricting employers' access to employees' personal social media accounts, or the applicable social media platforms' terms of use.) Finally, companies should control employee access to company social media accounts and passwords, including by taking steps to prevent individual employees from changing account usernames or passwords without authorization.

*December 2013*

*About the authors and firm

Aaron Rubin is a partner and Anelia Delcheva is an associate in the Technology Transactions Group at Morrison & Foerster LLP, a global law firm with 17 offices in the United States, Europe, and Asia. In addition, Mr. Rubin is a co-editor of, and Ms. Delcheva is a contributor to, Socially Aware, the firm's Burton Award-winning guide to the law and business of social media (http://www.sociallyawareblog.com). This article does not constitute legal advice and the views expressed herein shall not be attributed to Morrison & Foerster LLP or its clients.

# Chapter 33

## How Flexible Are You? Stretching the Boundaries with a Remote Workforce

by Laura Hayward and Brian Morris*

Yahoo! CEO Marissa Mayer's recent decision to ban telecommuting has highlighted the issue of how employers of all sizes respond to technological changes that are redefining the workplace.

In addition to the savings of decreased overheard (in the form of office space, equipment, or otherwise), telecommuting may provide other tangible benefits. Indeed, recent studies suggest telecommuting may increase employee satisfaction,[1] decrease turnover (and consequently, recruiting and new employee training costs),[2] and decrease absenteeism.[3] It can also reduce an employer's "carbon footprint" by eliminating the energy consumption associated with traveling to the workplace. However, these technological changes also impact how supervisors and subordinates interact, and the human component may lag behind technological advances. A recent MIT study, for instance, found that supervisors often look more favorably upon employees who put in "face time."[4]

From the startup employer to the multinational corporation, the potential to telecommute creates new compliance challenges. For employers that decide not to offer telecommuting, working from home might remain a "reasonable accommodation" under state and federal disability laws that these employers must still consider. Employers offering telecommuting should ensure their confidential data and intellectual property remain uncompromised. Monitoring the "work time" of telecommuting employees, especially for those paid on an hourly basis, creates its own set of difficulties. These are but a few of the issues employers will wrestle with in adapting to technological innovation that allows employees to work from anywhere in the world. Proactively maintaining and periodically updating alternative working arrangements or telecommuting policies is essential to realizing the benefits, and avoiding the pitfalls, of the changing workplace.

## Telecommuting and the American Workplace

The relationship of the employee to the physical workplace is rapidly changing. The U.S. Census Bureau reports that in 2010 13.4 million American workers worked from home at least 1 day per week.[5] This is up approximately 18 percent from 2005 (despite a two percent drop in the number of individuals employed) and constitutes nearly 10 percent of the American workforce.[6] Moreover, home-based work for those employed in engineering, the computer industry, and science increased by 69 percent from 2000 to 2010.[7] The western United States has the highest percentage of home-based workers (11.4 percent), perhaps partially due to its burgeoning startup culture.

In industries where telecommuting is common, permitting employees to work remotely may become a competitive necessity. In other industries, it may be a way to gain a competitive advantage. Either way, human resources staff and legal counsel should carefully manage the transition and day-to-day implementation of remote working arrangements.

## Legal Complications

### *Work "Away from Work" and Equal Employment Opportunity*

Not all workplaces are well-suited to work-from-home arrangements. The technological ability to work remotely, however, may create obligations under the Americans with Disabilities Act and related state laws; namely, "work from home" can in some circumstances arguably constitute a reasonable accommodation.[8] The Equal Employment Opportunity Commission adopts this position and contends that work from home/telecommuting arrangements may be a reasonable accommodation even if working remotely is not available to other employees.[9] Employers that wish to have a general policy against telecommuting should keep in mind their potential obligations under state and federal disability laws. Moreover, they should be aware that entering into remote working arrangements with some employees may make denying such benefits to disabled employees more difficult.

Many employers offer telecommuting on an informal basis, but the absence of a formal policy can expose employers to potential discrimination lawsuits. Disparate use of managerial discretion in this regard may form the basis of disparate treatment or disparate impact allegations. Employers that maintain and evenly apply telecommuting policies are better positioned to avoid such claims.

### *Protecting Company Data*

Telecommuting can exacerbate the challenges employers face with respect to protecting sensitive data. For example, some employers permit remote employees to access and create confidential information on their personal devices. By doing so, employers are less able to ensure disgruntled employees do not retain and disseminate confidential or trade secret information post-termination. In addition, consumer electronic devices generally lack the security necessary to protect against malicious hacking. The legal framework surrounding employee privacy and employer access to dual-use employee-owned electronic devices is complicated, and warrants attention should an employer allow employees to work on personal devices.

Employers whose business requires that they maintain strict privacy controls and/or whose primary asset is intellectual property should consider policies requiring the use of company-owned equipment when accessing or creating sensitive information. Employers should also have established procedures for the return of company property upon termination of employment. Such policies can curb ex-employees' retention of private information, and inadvertent disclosure to third parties (such as spouses and housemates) who may share devices.

### *Wage and Hour Compliance*

A recent study found that employees who work from home add an average of 5 to 7 hours of productive time, often in addition to their standard workweek.[10] While remote employees' willingness to work beyond the standard 40-hour workweek makes telecommuting an attractive option for some employers, it comes with potential wage and hour complications.

The inability to monitor remote employees' schedules makes it more difficult to prohibit off-the-clock work and to ensure compliance with overtime regulations for non-exempt workers. In some states, employees are entitled to overtime for hours worked in excess of 8 hours in a day and/or for working seven consecutive days. Thus, employers should remain diligent in monitoring remote employees' schedules and working hours. In addition to overtime, employers should be aware of all applicable meal and rest break regulations and recordkeeping requirements in all jurisdictions in which they operate. The reality is that remote working arrangements require engaged human resources staff to closely monitor wage and hour compliance.

**Is Telecommuting Right for Your Business?**

Whether telecommuting and other flexible arrangements are good for a particular workplace is contextual. Employers considering these options should take heed of Yahoo!'s experience. Some news sources are reporting that Yahoo!'s decision to end telecommuting came after examining VPN logs which showed that many remote employees were not signing in.[11] This shows that employers should not fall into an "out of sight, out of mind" mentality for both business and legal reasons. Moreover, the backlash against Mayer suggests that it is difficult to undo a corporate culture accustomed to flexibility and minimal oversight of its working arrangements. This, in turn, highlights the importance of being compliance-minded from the outset. Startups and growing companies are uniquely situated to mold a culture that helps remote employees remain productive even as they grow in size, and are accustomed to working with a compliance-minded management team.

**Next Steps**

This article discusses only a few of the many challenges created by the remote workplace. To capture the maximum benefits of a well-functioning remote workforce, employers should consider other issues, such as workers' compensation, occupational safety and health, and state taxation. Thus, employers of all sizes can benefit from conferring with experienced employment counsel to evaluate their existing remote working arrangements, or to implement new ones. In addition, employers informally offering remote work options should create formal written policies.

Proactive employers will be well positioned to adapt to the workplace of tomorrow—where boundaries are not defined by the traditional walls of an office.

*March 2013*

*<u>About the authors and firm</u>

Littler is the largest global employment and labor law practice with more than 1,000 attorneys in over 60 offices worldwide. Littler represents management in all aspects of employment and labor law and serves as a single source solution provider to the global employer community.

Laura Hayward is a Shareholder, and Brian Morris is an Associate, in Littler Mendelson's San Francisco office. If you would like further information, please contact Ms. Hayward at lhayward@littler.com, or Mr. Morris at bmorris@littler.com.



<u>Endnotes</u>

1. Nicholas Bloom, James Liang, John Roberts, and Zhichun Jenny Ying, *Does Working From Home Work? Evidence From A Chinese Experiment*, Stanford University, Feb. 22, 2013.

2. *Id.*

3. Peter J. Mateyka and Melanie A. Rapino, United States Census Bureau, P70-132, *Home-Based Workers in the United States: 2010* (Oct. 2012).

4. Kimberly Elsbach and Daniel Cable, *Why Showing Your Face at Work Matters*, MIT Sloan Management Review (Summer 2012).

5. Neil Shah, *More Americans Working Remotely*, The Wall Street Journal, March 5, 2013, *available at* http://online.wsj.com.

6. *See supra* note 3.

7. *Id.*

8. *See Nixon-Tinkelman v. N.Y.C. Dep't of Health & Mental Hygiene*, 434 Fed. App'x 17 (2d Cir. 2011) (remanding to the district court to consider, *inter alia*, whether working from home is a reasonable accommodation).

9. Equal Employment Opportunity Commission, *Work At Home/ Telework as a Reasonable Accommodation.*

10. Marcy C. Noonan and Jennifer L. Glass, *The hard truth about telecommuting*, Monthly Labor Review (June 2002).

11. Brett Molina, *Report: VPN logs led to Yahoo telecommute*, USA Today, March 6, 2013.

# Chapter 34
# Workplace Wellness Programs

by John B. Brescher, Jr., Mark A. Daniele, Joel E. Horowitz, Jane S. Kimball and Eleanor D. Thompson*

## Introduction

Recognizing that unhealthy lifestyles affect people of all ages, including those in the workforce, employers are using legally sanctioned incentives in an attempt to change behavior toward better and healthier choices through Workplace Wellness Programs. The expected collateral benefits are reduced costs to the employer due to healthier employees who use fewer health services, employees who are more productive at work and employees who lose less time from work. Specifically, these programs are designed to promote health and prevent disease by reducing or eliminating a sedentary lifestyle, bad eating habits, tobacco use and alcohol consumption and in so doing reduce or eliminate chronic diseases, such as diabetes, heart disease, respiratory conditions, etc. The Patient Protection and Affordable Care Act (ACA) promotes Workplace Wellness Programs; some large employers have already implemented Workplace Wellness Programs, but their positive impact on employee health and employer costs is disputed at this time and may require more time to accurately assess.

## New Regulations

https://www.federalregister.gov/articles/2013/06/03/2013-12916/incentives-for-nondiscriminatory-wellness-programs-in-group-health-plans

New regulations were issued jointly by the Department of Health and Human Services (HHS), the Department of Labor (DOL) and the Department of the Treasury (Treasury) on May 29, 2013, titled "Incentives for Nondiscriminatory Wellness Programs in Group Health Plans" (26 CFR Part 54; 29 CFR Part 2590; 45 CFR Parts 146-147, June 3, 2013).

The regulations were effective August 2, 2013 and apply to group health plans for plan years beginning on or after January 1, 2014. These final regulations are designed to ensure nondiscrimination in their application, and to provide comprehensive guidance with respect to the general requirements for Workplace Wellness Programs while providing plans and issuers with flexibility to encourage innovations. Future sub-regulatory guidance will be forthcoming as necessary.

**Who Must Comply?**

The regulations apply to insured, self-insured, grandfathered and non-grandfathered group health plans. These Workplace Wellness Programs are administered by employers directly, through a vendor, through group health plans or through a combination, and all must comply.

Noncompliance can result in a civil action by regulators and/or a lawsuit by individual employees.

**Overview of Compliant Wellness Plans**

Workplace Wellness Programs are divided into two types of programs: the Participatory Programs and the Health-Contingent Programs.

**1. Participatory Programs**

The most popular programs adopted by employers, these plans will be deemed nondiscriminatory and in compliance with the ACA if they are made available to all similarly situated employees without regard to their health status. They are characterized by having either no reward or the reward not being conditioned on satisfying any standard that is related to a health factor. In other words, if a reward is given, it is not based on outcome.

Examples of Participatory Programs include gym membership, filling out a risk assessment, attending a health education seminar, or participating in diagnostic testing without the requirement of a specific result.

**2. Health-Contingent Programs**

Health-Contingent Programs are defined as those programs that require employees to satisfy a standard related to a health factor to earn a reward or to avoid a penalty. The new regulations create two separate categories for Health-Contingent Programs: Activity Only and Outcome-Based.

*Activity Only*

The employee is required to perform or complete an activity related to a health factor, regardless of the outcome, to attain the reward or avoid the penalty. Stated otherwise, the programs do not require an individual to attain or maintain a specific health outcome.

Examples include walking, dieting, attending an exercise program or attending a nutrition class. The employee need only complete the program to obtain the reward or avoid the penalty.

An alternative standard must be provided to individuals for whom it is unreasonably difficult because of a medical condition or medically inadvisable to meet the standard; for example, an individual is unable to participate in a walking program due to recent surgery or pregnancy, or as a result of asthma. The regulations provide safeguards to ensure individuals are given a reasonable opportunity to qualify for the reward. For those employees unable to perform or complete this program, their doctor may provide verification of the employee's medical condition that makes it unreasonable or dangerous for the employee to meet the standard. The doctor may also suggest an alternative standard, or the employer may choose to waive the standard and just provide the reward. A plan or issuer may seek verification, such as a statement from the individual's personal physician that a health factor makes it unreasonably difficult for the individual to satisfy, or medically inadvisable for the individual to attempt to satisfy the otherwise applicable standard in an activity-only wellness program, if reasonable under the circumstances.

*Outcome-Based*

The employee is required to possess or achieve a specific health outcome to attain the reward or avoid the penalty. Generally, these programs have progressive levels: first, a measurement, test, or screening as part of an initial standard; and then a larger program that targets individuals who do not meet the initial standard with wellness activities.

Examples include achieving a normal body mass index (BMI); attending an antismoking program and discontinuing smoking, attaining certain levels for cholesterol or glucose screenings, and meeting targets for exercise. The tools used to achieve the goals include using a health coach, taking a health fitness course, adhering to a health improvement action plan or complying with a health care provider's plan of care.

An alternative standard must be provided to any employee who does not meet the initial standard. For example, an education program or activity may be substituted. This is to ensure that the program is reasonably designed to improve health and is not a subterfuge for underwriting or reducing benefits based on health status. The employer cannot require an employee to provide physical verification of a need for an alternative standard under an outcome-based wellness program. However, if an individual's personal physician states that a standard is not medically appropriate for the individual, the plan or issuer must provide a reasonable alternative standard that accommodates the recommendations of the individual's physician with regard to medical appropriateness.

**Additionally, Health-Contingent Plan Requirements**

1. Give all eligible employees an opportunity to qualify for the reward or avoid the penalty at least once a year;

2. Provide a reward or absence of a penalty surcharge not in excess of 30%, or 50% if the program is designed to prevent or reduce tobacco use, calculated on the total cost of coverage (the combined total of the employer's and employee's contribution for employee-only coverage) under the employer's health plan; if dependents are eligible and participate, the percentage is calculated on the cost of coverage for dependents as well;

3. Be reasonably designed to promote health and prevent disease. The plan cannot be overly burdensome and cannot be used as a subterfuge for discrimination based on a health factor;

4. Make the full reward available to all similarly-situated individuals, which requires provision of a reasonable alternative standard or waiver of the original standard—another way to achieve the full reward for those individuals for whom it is unreasonably difficult or medically inadvisable

to satisfy the standard due to a medical condition. Alternative standards may be individualized or apply to an entire class of persons and may be themselves health-contingent, but they must be reasonably based on all facts and circumstances and the guidance of the regulations; and,

5. Reasonably disclose the availability of an alternative standard, or possible waiver, in program materials. The final rules provide sample language for alternative standards, including the availability of an alternative standard and required contact information.

**What Constitutes a Reward?**

A reward can be an incentive or a disincentive. For example, it can be a premium discount; a rebate on a premium or contribution; additional health benefits; modification to otherwise applicable cost sharing (deductible, copayment, coinsurance); other financial incentives; or the avoidance of a penalty, a premium surcharge or other financial disincentive.

**Agency Guidance**

The legal restrictions of the ACA, the Americans with Disabilities Act (ADA) and the Genetic Information Nondiscrimination Act (GINA) do not currently align. In order to maintain a nondiscriminatory workplace, several concerns need to be addressed by the Equal Employment Opportunity Commission (EEOC), including 1) whether in offering financial incentives/disincentives as a way to encourage participation in Workplace Wellness Programs, employers run afoul of the definition of "voluntary" in the ADA; 2) to what extent disabled, ill or older employees have the ability to secure a reasonable alternative standard to ensure eligibility for wellness program rewards; and, 3) whether disclosure of confidential qualifying health conditions employees have, including a family medical history, can be required as a condition of participation.

While the EEOC has accepted written testimony and held an open commission meeting on May 8, 2013, to discuss Workplace Wellness Programs, it has not issued guidance to employers and employees that would reconcile, clarify and/or definitively resolve current inconsistencies which exist between the ACA, the ADA and GINA. Guidance is required in order to allow employers to design and operate Workplace Wellness Programs that comply with all nondiscrimination and privacy provisions of the law and to allow employees to work in a nondiscriminatory workplace.

**Judicial Rulings**

The first legal challenge to Workplace Wellness Programs has been decided in favor of the employer by way of Summary Judgment Motion and affirmed by the 11th Circuit.

In the case of Seff v. Broward Co., 691 F3d 1221 (11th Cir. 2012), Broward County implemented a Workplace Wellness Program through its insurance carrier, Coventry Healthcare. The goal was to reduce health care costs. Specifically, employees were required to undergo a biometric screening exam and an online health risk assessment (HRA). Employees identified as suffering from any of five designated disease states were given access to a health coaching program. Participation was rewarded with a waiver from co-pays for medication prescribed in conjunction with the identified disease. A $20 biweekly surcharge was deducted from an employee's salary for failure to participate in the Workplace Wellness Program.

The employees brought a class action lawsuit alleging that requiring employees to undergo medical exams and provide medical information to their health care insurance carrier violated the ADA because of the penalty imposed for nonparticipation. Broward County argued that the Workplace Wellness Program was voluntary and complied with the ADA's safe harbor provision. The court granted Summary Judgment in favor of Broward County, ruling that the Workplace Wellness Program fell into the ADA's safe harbor and the 11th Circuit Court of Appeals affirmed, finding that the Workplace Wellness Program was a term of the benefit plan within the safe harbor and did not have to be identified in the plan's written documents.

A putative class action based on similar facts, that is, penalties imposed for failure of employees of the Oregon Department of Corrections and Oregon State Police to submit to an HRA, was filed in February 2012. It alleges violation of the ADA.

## Employer Acceptance of Wellness Plans

Surveys on the effectiveness of Workplace Wellness Programs have been performed over the years by Kaiser/HRET, Mercer Consulting, TowersWatson, etc. It has been reported that Workplace Wellness Programs are a common feature of employee benefit programs for large employers. According to a Rand Corporation study issued May 29, 2013, 62% of employers with 200 or more employees offer wellness programs. Unfortunately, to date, fewer than 20% of employees participate in these plans. Employers, not so much employees, believe that these programs have a positive net economic effect, namely, promoting health and preventing disease; cutting health care costs; decreasing the cost of employer-sponsored health insurance, as well as reducing sick leave, absenteeism, presenteeism, and workers' compensation claims. The driving logic is that if the rewards are effective, health care costs will be reduced as an individual's health improves. However, the Rand Corporation report released on May 29, 2013 reports in its research findings that wellness programs have a very limited effect on the health of employees or the reduction of health care costs.

It is clear that more formal evaluation of the impact of Workplace Wellness Programs is required. Although employers are reported to have evaluated some metrics, most employers reportedly do not know the return on investment (ROI) and/or the sustainability of results. The administration takes the position that there is currently insufficient broad-based evidence, which makes it difficult to definitively assess the impact of Workplace Wellness Programs on health outcome and cost, although overall, employers largely report that Workplace Wellness Programs in general are delivering on their intended objectives of improving health and reducing cost. While data may not yet be conclusive, the future success of Workplace Wellness Programs will be governed by employers' cost-benefit analyses.

## Conclusion

Will Workplace Wellness Programs put companies at risk for lawsuits? Claims by employees can include discrimination, violation of medical privacy, violation of benefits reporting requirements and tax obligation, and breach of collective bargaining agreements. Despite these risks, these programs offer you an opportunity to enhance or implement new and effective ways to potentially reduce your health care costs and improve the lifestyles and productivity of your workforce.

*November 2013*

*About the authors and firm

In continuous business for more than 170 years, McCarter & English, LLP represents Fortune 500, mid-market and emerging growth companies in sophisticated transactions and multijurisdictional litigation. Its 400 attorneys are based in offices in Boston, Hartford, New York, Newark, Philadelphia, Stamford, Washington, D.C., and Wilmington. Visit http://www.mccarter.com to learn more. For information regarding the contents of this publication, please contact Mark A. Daniele, Partner and Chair of the Tax, Employee Benefits and Private Clients Practice Group, at (973) 639-2090 or mdaniele@mccarter.com.

Disclaimer by McCarter & English, LLP: This publication is for informational purposes only and is not offered as legal advice regarding any particular matter. No reader should act on the basis of this publication without seeking appropriate professional advice.

# Chapter 35

## Workplace Violence Examined

by Kelly O. Scott, Esq.*

What can employers do to prevent workplace violence? Unfortunately, we have learned a lot about violence, but we can use that knowledge to our advantage. In order for an employer to implement preventative measures, it must first understand workplace violence itself, both in terms of the types of violent acts that can occur as well as the risk factors associated with the various types of workplace violence. According to the federal Occupational Safety and Health Administration ("OSHA"), there are four types of workplace violence. The categories are as follows:

**Type I: Criminal Intent.** Violent acts committed by people who have entered the workplace to commit a robbery or other crime. Although these acts can be committed by current or former employees, the acting agent typically has no legitimate business relationship with the workplace and enters the affected workplace specifically to commit a criminal act;

**Type II: Customer/Client/Patients.** Violence directed at employees by customers, clients, patients, students, passengers, inmates, prisoners and others to whom the employer provides a service;

**Type III: Co-Worker.** Violence against co-workers, supervisors or managers committed by a current or former employee, manager or supervisor; and

**Type IV: Personal.** Violence in the workplace committed by a non-employee who has a relationship with an employee. This usually involves an assault of a current employee, supervisor or manager by a current or former spouse, lover, relative or friend or some other person who has a dispute with an employee of the affected workplace.

OSHA can also tell us who is at risk. High-risk industries include healthcare and social services settings, such as hospitals, clinics, pharmacies, home health agencies, alcohol and drug treatment providers and social welfare service providers. In addition, small, late-night retail establishments are considered to be high-risk establishments. Schools where students have a history of violent behavior and certain other types of service providers such as justice system personnel, customer service representatives and delivery personnel are also frequently at risk.

Type I events often occur during the commission of a robbery when an employee or proprietor is killed or injured. These events typically occur at small, late-night retail venues, but no retail store is immune from the possibility of a robbery. Retail robberies usually occur between the hours of 11:00 p.m. and 6:00 a.m. and are most often carried out by persons armed with a gun or knife. Additional factors that put retail employees at risk include the exchange of money and availability of valued items such as jewelry, 24-hour operation, solo or isolated work sites, the sale of alcohol and poorly lit stores and parking areas. Among small, late-night retail establishments, liquor stores, gas stations and convenience stores are common targets.

Type I events represent the most common type of fatal workplace violence event, but Type II events involving victims who provide services to the public are increasing. In addition, non-fatal Type II events involving assaults to service providers, particularly within the healthcare industry, may represent the most prevalent category of workplace violence resulting in physical injury. However, any business working with patients, clients, passengers, customers or students known or suspected to have a history of violence is at risk.

More common Type II assaults are inflicted upon public safety and correctional personnel, transportation providers, teachers, sales personnel and others who work in the public or private service sector who provide professional, public safety, administrative or business services to the public. According to Cal/OSHA, Type I events represent irregular occurrences in the life of any particular at-risk establishment, while Type II events can occur on a more regular basis in many service establishments and therefore represent a more pervasive risk for such service providers.

Type III and Type IV events are often more difficult to understand and may, at first, defy reasonable explanation. While these events can attract significant media attention, they are actually less common in occurrence than Type I or Type II events. Type III or Type IV events usually involve a single employee, supervisor or manager as the primary target of the assailant. The individual is often seeking revenge for what he or she perceives as unfair treatment by such person or persons. Employees with a history of assault or who have exhibited belligerent, intimidating or threatening behavior to others are among the risk factors for a Type III event. Although Type III and Type IV events can lead to fatalities, the most prevalent type of event usually involves threats or other types of verbal harassment.

Every employer should perform an initial assessment to identify workplace security factors that might contribute to violence in the workplace and consider preventative measures. Using the risk factors outlined above, and with consideration to the various types of possible workplace violence and the nature of the employer's business, employers should establish various workplace security measures as part of an Injury and Illness Prevention Program ("IIPP"). Indeed, in California, employers at risk for the various types of violence are required by Cal/OSHA to include as part of their business's IIPP the following:

1. A system for ensuring that employees comply with safe and healthy work practices, including ensuring that all employees comply with work practices designed to make the workplace more secure and refrain from engaging in threats or physical actions which create a security hazard to other employees in the workplace;

2. A system for communicating with employees in a form readily understandable about workplace security hazards, including a means an employee can use to inform the employer of security hazards at the worksite without fear of reprisal;

3. Procedures for identifying workplace security hazards, including scheduled periodic inspections to identify unsafe conditions and

work practices;

4. Procedures for investigating occupational injury or illness, including those arising from a workplace assault or threat of assault;

5. Procedures for correcting unsafe conditions, work practices and work procedures, including workplace security hazards, in a timely manner and based on the severity of the hazard and with attention to procedures for protecting employees from physical retaliation for reporting threats; and

6. Training and instruction on how to recognize workplace security hazards, measures to prevent workplace assaults and what to do when an assault occurs, including emergency action and post-emergency procedures.

Additional measures may be required depending on the nature of the business. For example, late-night retail stores are encouraged to remove clutter or other obstructions and signs from windows so that an unobstructed view of the store is possible. Keeping the store and parking lot brightly lit is a good idea, as is mounting mirrors and surveillance cameras to allow monitoring of otherwise hidden corners of the establishment. Limiting the amount of cash available and posting an appropriate sign regarding this fact is a helpful deterrent to robbery, as is training employees on what to do in the event a robbery actually occurs.

For establishments at risk for Type II events, controlling physical access through the workplace is an important preventative measure. Barriers between clients and service providers may be required. Alarm systems or "panic buttons" may be appropriate. Further, it is advisable to train employees on escape routes and establish a "buddy" system in the event of an actual emergency. The retention of security personnel should also be considered.

For Type III events, employers must monitor employees who have a history of assaults or who have exhibited belligerent, intimidating or threatening behavior. Cal/OSHA reports that an employer's considerate and respectful management of its employees represents an effective strategy for preventing Type III events. Layoffs, reductions in workforce and disciplinary actions can be triggering events and should be carried out in a manner which is designed to minimize the potential for the person to perceive the treatment as unfair or abusive. In connection with Type II, III and IV events, employers should consider seeking a temporary restraining order and an injunction on behalf of the affected employee(s) where appropriate.

In specific cases of workplace violence or threats of violence, employers are encouraged to seek legal counsel to ensure that the offense is responded to properly and that employees' safety is protected. In addition, employers should not hesitate to contact law enforcement when there has been an assault or serious threat of harm.

*September 2013*

*About the author and firm

Kelly O. Scott, Esq. is a partner at the law firm of Ervin, Cohen & Jessup LLP. The article is intended to present an overview of current legal trends and should not be construed as representing advice on specific, individual legal matters. 

Please direct any questions or comments regarding this article, to the author, Kelly O. Scott, at kscott@ecjlaw.com or 310.281.6348. Ervin Cohen & Jessup LLP is a full-service business law firm located in Beverly Hills, California. For more information please visit http://www.ecjlaw.com.

# About the Editors

**George J. Siedel** is the Williamson Family Professor of Business Administration and the Thurnau Professor of Business Law at the Ross School of Business, University of Michigan. He completed his graduate legal studies at Cambridge University and the University of Michigan.

**John V. Siedel** is President of Van Rye Publishing, LLC. He completed his graduate legal studies at the University of Iowa College of Law. Prior to attending law school he worked for the United States Department of Justice where he received a Special Commendation Award recognizing outstanding service during litigation.

Made in the USA
Monee, IL
04 November 2026

67387004R00144